rench origins of
English tragedy

Manchester University Press

French origins of English tragedy

Richard Hillman

Manchester University Press
Manchester and New York
distributed in the United States exclusively by Palgrave Macmillan

Copyright © Richard Hillman 2010

The right of Richard Hillman to be identified as the author of this work has been asserted by him in accordance with the Copyright, Designs and Patents Act 1988.

Published by Manchester University Press
Oxford Road, Manchester M13 9NR, UK
and Room 400, 175 Fifth Avenue, New York, NY 10010, USA
www.manchesteruniversitypress.co.uk

Distributed in the United States exclusively by
Palgrave Macmillan, 175 Fifth Avenue, New York,
NY 10010, USA

Distributed in Canada exclusively by
UBC Press, University of British Columbia, 2029 West Mall,
Vancouver, BC, Canada V6T 1Z2

British Library Cataloguing-in-Publication Data
A catalogue record for this book is available from the British Library

Library of Congress Cataloging-in-Publication Data applied for

ISBN   978 0 7190 8276 4   hardback

First published 2010

The publisher has no responsibility for the persistence or accuracy of URLs for any external or third-party internet websites referred to in this book, and does not guarantee that any content on such websites is, or will remain, accurate or appropriate.

Typeset in 10/12pt Arno Pro
by Graphicraft Limited, Hong Kong
Printed in Great Britain
by TJ International Ltd, Padstow

For Pauline – 'the sweet'st companion'

Contents

Acknowledgements		*page* viii
Textual note		ix
1	Introduction	1
2	On the generic cusp: *Richard II*, *La Guisiade* and the invention of tragic heroes	16
3	Out of their classical depth: from pathos to bathos in early English tragedy; or, the comedy of terrors	33
4	Staging the Judith jinx: heads or tales?	62
Works cited		97
Index		105

Acknowledgements

These are mostly of a general nature but no less important for that – on the contrary. Since I took up my position in Tours at the Université François-Rabelais and its Centre d'Études Supérieures de la Renaissance in 2001, my long-standing interest in French-English connections in the early modern period has received fresh impetus and met with new opportunities for expression within both research and pedagogical structures. (Both sorts of structure, sadly, are seriously menaced at present by a round of so-called reforms to the French university system.) Much of the material in this book has been adapted from papers first presented, in English or French, at conferences organized by receptive colleagues. I am particularly grateful to the Tudor Theatre Round Table (CESR – CNRS, Université de Tours), the Équipe Littératures et Sociétés Anglophones (MRSH, Université de Caen), and the Institut de Recherches sur la Renaissance, l'Âge Classique et les Lumières (CNRS, Université Paul-Valéry – Montpellier III) for providing me with ample and congenial platforms. As a result of the Montpellier conference, moreover, a version of part of Chapter 4 appears in another publication of Manchester University Press: *A Knight's Legacy: Mandeville and Mandevillian Lore in Early Modern England*, edited by Ladan Niayesh (2010).

Textual note

Except where otherwise indicated, Shakespeare's works are cited, using the standard abbreviations, from *The Riverside Shakespeare*, gen. eds G. Blakemore Evans and J. J. M. Tobin, 2nd edn (Boston: Houghton Mifflin, 1997).

1

Introduction

This project applies to tragic patterns and practices a long-standing critical preoccupation of mine: the dynamic imaginative engagement of late sixteenth- and early seventeenth-century English dramatists and audiences with French texts and contexts.[1] As I have previously argued, that engagement is founded on historical causes, cultural as well as political, but sustained by the continuing imbrication of England's most pressing national and religious concerns with French ones.[2] It is also, paradoxically, an engagement that testifies, from the broad historical perspective, to a process of disengagement. English and French nationhood, for the first time since the Norman Conquest, are each now struggling towards self-definition, independently of the other (that is, the Other).

Even in retrospect, it is not possible to be precise about this process or absolute about its result: indeed, moments of particular tension – over the Anglo-American war in Iraq, over social and economic policy within the European Community, over the Olympic Games – are still capable of resonating with the intense historical interdependency of French and English identities. But it remains a fair generalization to state that by the mid-seventeenth century, those identities had become distinctly consolidated to the point where 'modern' assumptions about international difference govern the discourses of each country in relation to the other. By contrast, the hundred years or so with which I am concerned enacted the complex mechanisms of differentiation, and did so across unusually profound systemic changes: the evolution from feudalism to capitalism, the fragmentation of the monolithic medieval Church, the contested concentration of monarchic power, the virtual abandonment, step by reluctant step, of England's territorial pretensions in France. During this period, the English, like the French, still found it difficult to conceive of themselves without taking the other/Other into account. Conversely, to look across the Channel was also invariably to see oneself, as in a mirror, but to see oneself constantly in flux, evanescent, receding from the secure hold afforded by fixed ideas or comforting stereotypes. This is why, in *Shakespeare, Marlowe and the Politics of France* (2002), I found useful as a background metaphor for national self-definition the Lacanian idea of personal subjectivity as experienced, in the 'mirror stage', through the 'aphanisis' or 'fading' of the image of the self.

It is my working hypothesis that we more fully recover the multiple and dynamic engagement of early modern English thinking with its French Other by resisting forms of compartmentalization largely imposed retrospectively, and along the axes of modern academic disciplines. The separation of national literatures, of 'literature' itself from other discursive forms, of religion from politics, of 'history' and 'science' from both – these, too, are processes uneasily underway in the early modern period and far from fully realized. Equally inchoate is the development of a notion of authorship that, at least from the Romantic period, will bolster itself by hiving off the concepts of originality, source and influence. My approach to texts and contexts here continues to presume the circulation and co-presence of diverse discourses within a common cultural space – hence, at once the validity and the value of relating them intertextually, rather than attempting to prove relationships of source and influence according to quasi-judicial principles.

Paradoxically, such an approach occasionally produces surprising 'discoveries' that may or may not stand up in the eye of the beholder – that is, according to the rules of evidence that the beholder sees fit to apply. Some readers may consider that disappointingly few such moments are generated here in proportion to the amount of intertextual detail supplied, much of which emanates from sources alien to scholars of English literature (sources, moreover, sometimes well outside the canons established by Renaissance French specialists). I can respond only that, although I have tried to render that material as accessible and engaging as possible, my primary objective has not been to supplement the research of dozens of learned editors, or, notably, of Geoffrey Bullough (1957–75) on Shakespeare, but rather at once to enlarge and refine, by a process of intertextual tracing, the common cultural space in question. The purpose is to sharpen the beholder's perception on the whetstone of early modern practices of reading and writing. My working assumption has been that if a text had been printed, whenever and wherever, it might have been accessible to any literate person for reading, while at a few points I have evoked the possibility of personal networks, typically constituted on political and/or religious lines, through which manuscripts may have circulated. These principles are widely accepted as applying within national and linguistic boundaries. Scholarship has not been in the habit, however, of redrawing those boundaries to include both sides of the Channel. I have tried to do so, sometimes in ways that allow, if only hypothetically, for what might be called a professional interest on a dramatist's part.

Thanks to generations of scholarly industry, we know enough about Shakespeare's working habits, in particular, to state with some confidence that, when developing a play on a given subject, he normally consulted a wide range of more-or-less closely related material, dramatic and otherwise. If one presupposes a moderate competence in French – a point I take up in *French Reflections* – it thus seems reasonable to hypothesize his interest, say, in the dramatic treatments of Roman themes across the Channel; there is then no reason to exclude from the field of vision any French tragedy of Cleopatra prior to his own, certainly not on the grounds of its present obscurity. In fact, the *Cléopâtre* of Nicolas de Montreux (1594–95), though virtually unknown today, had a particular claim to attention in its own time, given its author's contemporary prominence and active ultra-Catholic politics, and I therefore include it in an exploration of French theatrical precursors when I turn my attention to Shakespeare's tragedy as a 'case study' in French-English intertextuality.[3]

To invoke common elements is to run the risk of dabbling in commonplaces. On the other hand, to deal in commonplaces is not necessarily to dabble; indeed, the latter may serve to define more fully the cultural space in question: that *common place* has, after all, its gross dimensions, as well as its more obscure angles and corners. Moreover, commonplaces may carry meaning not merely in themselves – that is, as documentation of shared intellectual patterns – but through their contexts and applications. And their resonances may thereby become quite particular.

This effect emerges in various forms across the following chapters, although it comes most fully into its own in the more extended explorations undertaken in *French Reflections*. Indeed, I dwell there on a textual instance so familiar – Hamlet's evocation of the 'special providence in the fall of a sparrow' (*Ham.*, V.ii.219–20) – that it may as well serve here concisely to make a broad methodological point. My argument, conducted along a series of intertexts, is that by the time Shakespeare deployed that biblically derived commonplace to show the Prince anticipating the fatal fencing match, it had become tightly bound up in the cultural imagination with a moment in recent French political and religious history that mattered a great deal to Elizabethans: namely, a treacherous royal attempt on the life of Antoine de Bourbon, First Prince of the Blood and King of Navarre, father of the reigning Henri IV.

The point depends on recognizing that for a brief, precarious and highly fraught moment around 1560, Antoine had seemed to offer hope not only that

Protestantism might prevail in France – the promise associated with his son in more sustained fashion – but also that civil war might be avoided. To pursue the historical parallel – as is done at some length, given that modern readers are not generally familiar with the facts or their textual representations – is to activate hitherto unsuspected material resonances at the very level of the play most widely considered to reflect Shakespeare's 'pure invention': the character of his protagonist. Against this background, Hamlet's commonplace tag, otherwise a smooth fit with the intellectual and discursive 'grammar' of the text, reveals itself as what theory sometimes labels an 'ungrammaticality', a signal of intertextual presence.[4]

Such, in brief, is the analytical premise and method of this two-volume project, as it was of *Shakespeare, Marlowe and the Politics of France*. It is an approach that, when the criteria establishing 'influence' cannot necessarily be met to the satisfaction of the majority, still seems to me the best alternative to confining potentially meaningful and historically feasible textual juxtapositions at the level of museum curiosities, with the cautionary label attached, 'Do not touch.' Obviously, risks are being run, but these arguably boil down to the universal (and usually immeasurable) one of criticism generally: that of being beside the point. To propose ways in which audiences or readers might have made sense of such juxtapositions may finally be less assertive and more straightforward than simply to rank textual relations according to hierarchical categories such as Bullough's ('source', 'probable source', 'possible source', 'analogue') and expect them to speak for themselves.

I

I now shift the ground from method to content – the generic orientation that definitively disqualifies the present book as itself a sequel. In so far as *Shakespeare, Marlowe and the Politics of France* was concerned with the construction and representation of nationhood, it positioned itself as a modest complement to such major studies of early modern English self-definition as those of Richard Helgerson (1992) and, more recently, Michael Neill (2000) – works in which, despite their impressive scale and scope, the formative French connection seemed to me neglected. Accordingly, my work focused on plays of the 1590s whose purport was the staging of English history, and which thereby lent themselves to a double interplay of meanings: between English and French, between past and present.

By contrast, the material I have gathered for this study coheres generically in a way that bears on contemporary notions of tragedy. At least initially, this was more by accident than by design, but I found that the French echoes and models I was tracking tended to carry and impart generic significance. The reason, I believe, is that tragedy, while obviously of prestige and importance on both the public and private stages of London, was a relative novelty in England and remained formally ill- (or variously) defined, hence, in search of both matter and meaning. It had been, after all, *terra incognita* for English dramatists prior to the 1560s. Perhaps precisely because its only truly obligatory feature in English practice was a more-or-less bloody ending, it remained open-ended as a genre – almost infinitely flexible with regard to all sorts of variables: political content, the neo-Aristotelian 'unities', the extent of on-stage action, the use of the chorus, the role of higher powers, the mingling of kings and clowns, the shuttling between verse and prose, and the representation of the tragic hero, who might even be of less than noble rank. Paradoxically, given the formal allegiance of French Humanist tragedy itself to rigid constraints, such flexibility on the English side appears to have led tragic authors to draw on French source material and dramatic models without overmuch regard for consistency.

In Chapter 2, I take up Shakespeare's *Richard II*, a play which naturally figured also in *Shakespeare, Marlowe and the Politics of France*; I even return to a previous preoccupation: its relation to the virulently propagandistic *La Guisiade* (1589) of Pierre Matthieu, the future historiographer of Henri IV who was, at the time, an uncompromising partisan of the ultra-Catholic *Sainte Ligue*. My concern now, however, is quite specifically with Shakespeare's play as tragedy rather than as history. (After all, it alternatively carried, in its earliest editions, both generic labels.) I particularly want to consider what the French precursor has to show us about the phenomenon of the psychologically self-destructive tragic hero – a notable innovation at this point in the evolution of the English tradition.

This phenomenon, in fact, makes one of three tragic paradigms which, in the first phase of this project, I propose to focus on through pre-existing French lenses. Chapter 3 takes up some applications of classicism in both form and content, with special attention to the production of political meanings. Chapter 4 is concerned with confrontations between the warrior-hero and the *femme fatale*. It is not my intention to privilege Shakespeare in these chapters – the features in question belong to the genre at large – but he naturally receives a great deal of attention. (The emphasis and approach change in *French Reflections*, where successive chapters are each built round a Shakespearean text, which then attracts a range of French intertexts – dramatic, narrative, and otherwise – for avowedly interpretative purposes.)

I make no claim for my discussions, and least of all for my specific textual choices, as either exhaustive or exclusive. Far from talking the subject to death, I hope to have delineated areas and methods of investigation that will continue to appeal to researchers. At the same time, I cheerfully concede that any number of case studies would hardly add up to a comprehensive argument for the derivation from French sources of early modern English tragedy as a composite theatrical phenomenon. That is not my brief – there is no exclusive article ('the') in my title – nor would I expect successive scholarship to validate it. What I may hope for is merely sufficient supplementation, from sufficiently diverse points of view, to generate a partial revisionist history of the period's English drama.

I hasten to acknowledge as well that the conspicuous absence of a French equivalent of the London commercial stage in the sixteenth century reduces the available field of dramatic influence to a relatively few published plays. Many of my French intertexts are non-dramatic, and I develop the special relation I have previously posited between English dramatic practice and French political writing of a kind likely to engage the English. At the same time, this is to throw into relief what survives of the French theatre of politico-religious propaganda, a sub-genre historically obscured by the neo-classical orientation of French criticism and under-represented by the handful of extant texts. That genre is now at least receiving recognition as such: Madeleine Lazard (1980, p. 82) points out that school plays, in particular – which were often open to a wide audience (though few were published) – thrived on religious controversy. And there remains at least one tantalizing glimpse of the way in which political urgency may sometimes have prevailed over tragic formalism: *Le Guysien*, by Simon Belyard (published 1592), actually stages the on-stage murder of the Duke of Guise in a scene which, I have argued elsewhere ('Marlowe's Guise', 2008), probably inspired Marlowe. Belyard's tragedy was certainly acted, by the way, as its author testifies (sig. Aii^v), and so may be added to the evidence accruing against Paul Lacroix's bald late nineteenth-century assertion – still being echoed in the 1960s (Deierhauf-Holsboer 1968, p. 36) – that theatrical activity throughout France abruptly and utterly ceased between the assassination of the Guises in 1588 and the fall of the Catholic League in 1596.

The dominant French Humanist drama on classical themes was also politically pertinent, if more elusively so (presumably often by design). I sight along this major axis, too, with a view to bringing out, if nothing more definite, a sense of the 'French' quality that authors and audiences might have attached to English tragedies on the same subjects. Above all, it seems important to stress that the English of the turn of the sixteenth century did not have the benefit of that critical hindsight which has imaginatively constructed – largely on the blueprints of Shakespeare, on the one side, Corneille and Racine on the other – two stereotypically opposed theatrical edifices, 'Whose high, upreared, and abutting fronts / The perilous narrow ocean parts asunder' (*H5*, Pro.21–22):

Introduction

one disproportioned, in some places ramshackle, in others renovated in different styles, but with many entrances and lavishly hospitable; the other impeccably regular in appearance and well crafted, but stern and uninviting. That is the view of an aerial postcard (indeed, it is decidedly post-cardesian), and it is not particularly true to either landscape. Neglected on the French side are not only the sporadically recorded political and sensationalistic dramatic productions of the latter half of the sixteenth century but also the profusely documented tragicomedy of the earlier seventeenth. The latter tradition should impress scholars of English at least for making possible André Mareschal's astonishingly vivid stage adaptation (prior to 1640) of a large chunk of Sidney's *Arcadia*.

I am far from depreciating the unparalleled dynamism and self-sufficiency of the early modern English theatrical enterprise. Indeed, that phenomenon constitutes a composite effect at once so vigorous, so diverse, and so (literally) unruly as arguably to preclude responsibly attributing it to single or dominant causes, *pace* some 'historicizing' criticism. However, its openness to virtually any and all things theatrically exploitable is demonstrably part of its diversity, and it is my contention that France served as a privileged major supplier of such commodities.

It occupied this position, I continue to maintain, for complex cultural and historical reasons, but I am no longer concerned directly with tracing how representations of France and Frenchness signify for the English and their Englishness. Instead, these studies in tragedy aim to follow more elusive processes of cultural absorption and transformation across the middle ground as it opens out intertextually on both sides of the Channel. Hence, I have decided not to include the handful of extant English plays that actually make tragedy out of French historical subjects – essentially the œuvre of Chapman, fascinating as it is, and indeed ineluctable in terms of English/French symbolic relations. To have included Chapman's French tragedies would have meant a split in the basic approach, and I have preferred to take them up separately elsewhere, as a coda to my previous treatment of English theatre and 'the politics of France'.[5]

II

The intertextual relationships indicated in this study imply a wider familiarity than is usually assumed on the part of English playwrights with published French texts of various kinds – historical, poetic, dramatic. With this would naturally go a certain sense of how various French texts related to each other, and some degree of sensitivity – however difficult it is to measure – to their social and political contexts. While allowing for the undoubted ignorance and prejudices of large segments of the theatre-going public, I prefer to posit at least some audience members for whom such distinctions would be meaningful.

With regard to compositional practice, too – that is, the question of how a range of 'French material' was used in practical ways – I would make the case for inclusiveness and flexibility as being the norm. In spite of post-Romantic, post-Freudian, and postmodern models of writing, we still tend to picture early modern dramatists as making conscious and coherent choices among sources for particular elements, even if they commonly drew on several in composing a single work. Often, by contrast, I detect a sort of *bricolage* or patching together of more than one 'source', sometimes including English translations and their originals (Marlowe's *Tamburlaine* material may be a case in point – see Chapter 4) even for the same element. This is a technique that thrives on effects of association, juxtaposition and superposition, and which accordingly resists, not only cut-and-dried conclusions, but all teleological analysis. A playwright, that is, sometimes used a variety of materials for the part of the job immediately at hand without necessarily aiming at a harmonious effect, at least of a kind suiting critical posterity's ideas of artistic unity or purity. In such cases, the variety of origins remains in suspension, as part of the epistemological background, until precipitated into semiotic play by a triggering 'ungrammaticality' which a critic can only hypothesize – preferably with supporting evidence – on behalf of an audience.

Further, it seems likely that an extraneous analogue or association sometimes determined which features of an obvious 'source' would be retained or exploited. What might be termed the Myth of the Single Source stands with difficulty when the apparatus of intertextual analysis may be deployed with some precision – albeit, again, hypothetically. Such is the case when a third text seems likely to have been engaged by an element traceable to a familiar origin but nevertheless felt as anomalous ('ungrammatical'). A concise instance – one, as it happens, that bears on the casting of a tragic shadow within Shakespeare's most actively 'French' history play – is furnished by the crime for which Pistol seeks to excuse the condemned Bardolph in *Henry V*:

> Fortune is Bardolph's foe, and frowns on him;
> For he hath stol'n a pax, and hanged must 'a be –
> A damned death!
> Let gallows gape for dog, let man go free,
> And let not hemp his windpipe suffocate.
> But Exeter hath given the doom of death
> For pax of little price.
>
> (III.vi.39–45)

As editors point out, this incident obviously derives from Henry's execution of a soldier for stealing a 'pyx', as reported by Holinshed; it thus testifies to the king's recorded rigour in the matter of discipline and special strictures against the robbing of churches. The (almost literally ungrammatical) substitution of 'pax' for 'pyx' has traditionally been treated as an error—whether Pistol's or Shakespeare's. Yet, on the reasonable presumption that it represents the text as performed, criticism has more recently endowed it with ironic functionality: after all, the English king finally imposes on the French a 'peace' of doubtful value that they nevertheless 'must buy' (V.ii.70), while his reason for restraining his troops is less than altruistic – in the historical sources, as, explicitly, in the play: 'when lenity and cruelty play for a kingdom, the gentler gamester is the soonest winner' (III.vi.112–13).[6]

At least some members of the 1599 audience, however, might well have had their perception enriched with further irony by the reminiscence (turning on the issue of 'little price', not mentioned in Holinshed) of a translated account of unruly soldiers pillaging a French church, an account that had been published just in the previous year: 'they cut the cord that sustained the pixe, to see whither it were siluer and gilt or no, but finding that it was but brasse, they threw it in despite against the ground.'[7] The episode forms part of an extended composite narrative of the French civil wars, *An historical collection, of the most memorable accidents, and tragicall massacres of France, vnder the raignes of Henry. 2. Francis. 2. Charles. 9. Henry. 3. Henry. 4. now liuing*. This volume is generally attributed to Jean de Serres but was probably compiled by the Swiss-based Calvinist Simon Goulart, who will resurface in both parts of this study as a spokesman for God's righteous judgement.[8]

It has been observed that the sections covering the reigns of Henri III and Henri IV derive from the *Histoire des derniers troubles de France* produced, beginning in 1594 with several re-editions, by the newly royalist Matthieu. This is the case only up to a point, however, and it is not from him that the compiler took a vivid account of the atrocities, ranging from rape to blasphemy, which were supposedly committed in 1589 at Saint Symphorien, a suburb of Tours, by the partisans of the Catholic League, taking advantage of the absence of the King of Navarre.[9] Whatever the source, the discourse engages with special point the taboo against robbing churches that applied in the contemporary code of warfare.[10] The immediate effect is at once to expose the cowardly hypocrisy of the ostentatiously pious *Ligueurs* and to present Navarre, though still a Protestant, as the answer to the entire French nation's need for order, honest dealing, and respect for both humanity and religion. But more profoundly implied is the metaphysical mechanism of offence and retribution set in motion by the enemies of God. As further instances in this study illustrate, the metaphorical application of 'tragedy', here introduced into the title by the anonymous translator, had yet to become casual, whether for Protestants or Catholics:[11] it would not be deemed a tragedy to be hit by a bus, except on the understanding that God, at whatever remove, was in the driver's seat.

There is further reason to suppose that Shakespeare's imagination might have been seized by *An historical collection* virtually at the moment of its publication, and in such a way as to accelerate the infusion of the historical record with tragic overtones. Shakespeare's two major historical works of 1599, *Henry V* and *Julius Caesar*, the latter frankly if ambiguously tragic, are increasingly recognized as mutually illuminating in both their dramatic method and their politics. Comparison is encouraged by the ambivalent reference to Henry as Caesar (and presumably as Essex)[12] by the Chorus introducing Act V (25 ff.). *An historical collection* (pp. 204–7) forcefully unfolds – in this, translating from Matthieu – the most extended formal comparison available between Caesar and Henri, Duke of Guise, who was assassinated on the orders of Henri III on 23 December 1588. The analogy itself was a commonplace, often used as a basis for aligning Rome's and France's subsequent troubles and lending itself to condemnation of overreaching, as when Michel Hurault virtually predicted Guise's violent end:

> the duke of Guize . . . is alreadie so farre in, that he must needs either be king, or be vndone altogither: there is no meane for him betweene these two extremities. *Marius, Cinna, Pompey, Lepidus,* and *Anthonie* may be examples hereof. As soone as a man hath aspired vnto tyranny, *Aut Cæsar aut nihil.* (*A discourse vpon the present estate of France*, 1588, p. 36)[13]

In keeping with the ambiguity of Shakespeare's Caesar, however, the analogy was equally adaptable to glorification. So Matthieu not only acknowledges ('the League called him her *Cæzar*, and made goodly comparisons betweene them' [Goulart 1598, p. 203]) but indeed reflects, in granting Guise many exceptional qualities. (The admiration of *La Guisiade* has not been wholly jettisoned.)

In any case, Matthieu's analysis of the political situation revolves – in ways that join Shakespeare's tragic treatment on the common ground of Plutarch – on the thematic axis of ambition, demagoguery and personal self-indulgence as self-destructive, as well as deleterious to the state. One striking point in common is the emotional frenzy whipped up in the people by the League's orators, including one who 'made his Auditorie weepe, by shewing the manner of this execution', another who strove 'to kindle and increase the fires of commotions' (p. 203). In Shakespeare, of course, as in the Life of Antony, it is the latter who, by way of the inflamed and inflammatory mob ('Go fetch fire' [III.ii.257]), takes up the Caesarean torch: 'Now let it work. Mischief, thou art afoot, / Take thou what course thou wilt' (260–61). Just so did Guise's Caesar-like combination of larger-than-life virtues and flaws guarantee 'the mischiefe and troubles of *France*' (p. 207). And while Shakespeare's fiery imagery may derive most directly from Plutarch in North's translation, his pivotal word 'mischief' does not. The concluding moral in *An historical collection* coincides closely, moreover, with that of the tragedy:

> And touching the end of the Duke of *Guise*, I say, that as the murther of the Dictator *Cæzar*, serued for a protext [sic] vnto *Anthony* & *Augustines*, to ouerthrow the Commonwealth of *Rome*: so this death of the Duke of *Guise*, put weapon into the hands of the Duke *de Maine*, like *Anthony*, to destroy both himselfe and his countrie. (Goulart 1598, p. 207)

The distinctly tragic cast of this commentary is absent, say, from the parallel in Hurault's updated *Excellent discourse* (1592), where the duc de Mayenne is simply described as drawing unexpected political profit from the death of his brother, 'In like manner as the murder of the *dictator Cæsar* serued for a pretence to *Antony* and *Augustus* to ouerthrowe the Romaine commonwealth' (sig. A3ᵛ [erroneously B3ᵛ]).

This is not to elevate *An historical collection* to the lofty status of 'source', although 'analogues' are clearly at issue. Simply, once the recently issued French compilation is taken into account, it becomes difficult indeed not to suspect Shakespeare of reading his Plutarch at this moment through and across it, and, more to the point, of encouraging his auditors to do the same. Thus, the uneasy evocation of the French civil wars that hovers behind the manifest English destiny of Henry V would become tinged with potentially disturbing lessons about the fine line between heroic leadership and demagoguery – between a 'band of brothers' (IV.iii.60) performing the 'will of God' (I.ii.259), as their (self-interested) bishops urge it upon them, and the *Sainte Ligue*. After all, the latter's argument for the royal entitlement of the House of Lorraine turned, no less than did that of Shakespeare's Canterbury, on the usurpation by Hugh Capet of 'the crown of Charles the Duke of Lorraine, sole heir male / Of the true line and stock of Charles the Great' (69–71).[14] That usurpation, in turn, runs parallel to the one effected by Henry's own father, which still provokes profound unease in his own relation to divine justice – witness his prayer on the eve of Agincourt (IV.i.92 ff.). Across the French intertext, the foreboding inherent in the image of London as joyfully receiving its 'conqu'ring Caesar' (V.Cho.28) attaches all the more persistently to the troubles instigated and subsequently endured by the House of Lancaster – troubles at once past and future: 'they lost France and made his England bleed, / Which oft our stage hath shown' (Epi.12).

III

This brief introduction has sought to sketch out a range of relations, which the ensuing chapters aim to fill in, between diverse French discourses and particular aspects of English tragedy. I conclude by proposing, nevertheless, that these relations are essentially historical rather than aesthetic – indeed, that they involve a form of historicism running deeper and more pervasively than that which seeks to isolate topical allusions or even cultural epistemes. The key to this fact is the imbrication of historical and political thinking in the early modern period with a religious – or, more broadly, metaphysical – perspective, certainly as the condition of the production of tragedy, on stage or off. It is on this ground that early modern English tragedy meets not only French religious polemic in various forms, but also Humanist theatre, sensationalistic narrative, and indeed the *entrée solennelle*, as I propose with regard to *All's Well* in *French Reflections*. Elizabethan tragedy can be most reductively defined as drama with death in it because death, for whomever the bell tolls, is always charged with significance. John Donne might not have become so famous for saying, 'any man's death diminishes me, because I am involved in mankind' (*Devotions*, 17 [Meditation], 1959, p. 109), had the filter of post-Romantic subjectivity not obscured the essentially medieval topos – the same commonplace that acquires particularity in Shakespeare's *Antony and Cleopatra*: when Caesar is observed to have been 'touch'd' by Antony's death, Maecenas replies, 'When such a spacious mirror's set before him, / He needs must see himself' (V.i.33, 34–35).

We tend to interpose another specious filter when we impose on even the most vehement of early modern polemics the category of 'propaganda'. Of course, the term is highly useful and nearly indispensable. But it has lost touch with its own early modern roots in the promotion of doctrinal truths and can convey only imperfectly the originating spirit of even the most blatant lies produced by the publicity machines of either the Catholic or Protestant factions (the latter notably including the English government).[15] Those machines presumed the constant and profound interpenetration of the material and the spiritual, of the human and the divine, that informed at once belief systems and cultural values – and that turned death into tragedy (or comedy, depending on point of view). Such a sense is not often reflected even in most of the recent criticism purporting to revalidate the importance of religion in early modern thought and literature. It is never neglected, by contrast, by one of the most illuminating current historians of sixteenth-century France, Denis Crouzet, little of whose major writing, perhaps significantly, has been translated into English.[16]

Crouzet appears to avoid the term 'propaganda' and so would probably not apply it, any more than I would, to, say, Marlowe's *Massacre at Paris*. This is hardly the same, however, as claiming that the play does not take sides (the Protestant one, in my view) – and consistently so; this is what made it tragedy for a contemporary audience, rather than the 'black farce' (Weil 1977, p. 91) that has largely gained the upper hand as a generic label in contemporary criticism. But I would insist, with Crouzet, that we should expand the concept of 'taking sides' so as to allow for the intensity and profundity of engagement that enabled, on the one hand, abrupt conversions (and reconversions), on the other, a willingness to die and to kill, to endure as well as to inflict the essential tragic experience – both in the most horribly cruel ways. Marlowe's 'atheism' should not be used as a convenient mechanism to place him above ideology; neither should his homosexuality. Any such transcendentalizing harks back to earlier recuperations of the author based on a post-Romantic concept of artistry, as when A. L. Rowse surveyed Marlowe's œuvre and magisterially pronounced: 'The appeal of *The Massacre*, after all, was only topical and superficial, and Marlowe was an artist. I don't suppose that *The Massacre* meant much more to him than it does to us' (1981, p. 101).

The scholarly challenge is, as always, redefining 'us', by at least identifying and partly clearing away the clutter of cultural interference. This can best be done by tracing, though the widest possible variety of texts, the ways in which contemporary French and English thought about themselves and each other. We cannot ever quite think the way they thought, but we can come closer by reading more of what they read. (This point will have to stand as justification for my sometimes extensive quotation of less accessible texts.) With regard to English dramatists, this means not presuming that they ventured into French territory only in search of untapped source material and when there was a dearth in their own language. We should cease resisting the evidence – provided, at the most basic level, by the language manuals – that many English men and women, representing an impressive variety of social positions, habitually had recourse, for all the reasons that belong to reading, to the vast body of published material available to them in French. And the latter, despite the vogue in restricted circles for Italian, remained by far the most widely and variously practised vernacular foreign language.[17]

It is certain that far fewer French people read or spoke English. On the other hand, there is hard evidence, if only tantalizing scraps of it, that English theatrical companies played in France at least in 1598, not only in Paris but in the provinces, and in 1604 (before the court at Fontainebleau).[18] Christian Biet, in introducing a recent collection of lesser-known sixteenth- and seventeenth-texts French texts entitled, *Théâtre de la cruauté* – some of the plays presented there would have a surprisingly familiar air for specialists in Elizabethan and Jacobean studies – goes so far as to situate this phenomenon within 'une relative internationalisation de l'espace et de la pratique dramatiques [a relative internationalization of dramatic space and practice]' (2006, p. xiv). Qualified though it is ('relative'), the claim is a large one – hence all the more enticing as an invitation to future research. Such research may at least be grounded on a firm cultural basis. For contemporary French writings on history and politics recurrently show that the French were also knowledgeable, and perhaps even more profoundly curious, about England and the English – for them too, the Other that reflected themselves.

Notes

1 The project, moreover, comes in two parts, with the present volume laying the conceptual and methodological foundations for another containing more sustained explorations, *French Reflections in the Shakespearean Tragic: Three Case Studies* (forthcoming).
2 See *Shakespeare, Marlowe and the Politics of France*, 2002, esp. pp. 1–29.
3 See *French Reflections*, Chapter 3. I argue for Shakespeare's knowledge of another of Montreux's plays in '*A Midsummer Night's Dream* and *La Diane* of Nicolas de Montreux', 2010.
4 For the origins of 'ungrammaticality' as a critical concept in the work of Michael Riffaterre, see esp. the latter's 'Sémiotique intertextuelle: l'interprétant', 1979, p. 134; 'Syllepsis', 1980 p. 627; and 'L'intertexte inconnu', 1981 p. 5. I have found the notion not only attractive in the abstract but practically productive ever since my frankly experimental study, *Intertextuality and Romance in Renaissance Drama* (1992), where my interest in sources first took on such a theoretical dimension.
5 See 'The Tragic Channel-Crossings of George Chapman, Part I: *Bussy D'Ambois* and *The Conspiracy and Tragedy of Byron*' (2004), and 'The Tragic Channel-Crossings of George Chapman, Part II: *The Revenge of Bussy D'Ambois* and *The Tragedy of Chabot*' (2005).
6 On Shakespeare's highly ironic adaptation of Holinshed as inflected by the discourses of the French Wars of Religion, see *Shakespeare, Marlowe and the Politics of France*, 2002, p. 192.
7 Goulart, *An historical collection*, 1598, p. 219; page numbers refer to the separately paginated section entitled, 'The First Book of the Historie of the last troubles of France, vnder the raignes of Henry the third, and Henry the fourth now liuing'.
8 On Goulart, see Jones 1917 (whose work is somewhat out of date, however), as well as Kingdon 1988, pp. 2–6. On responsibility for the original, commonly known as the *Histoire des cinq rois* but formally entitled, *Histoire des choses mémorables avenues en France, depuis l'an 1547 jusques au commencement de l'an 1597, sous le règne de Henri II, François II, Charles IX, Henri III et Henri IV, contenant infinies*

merveilles de notre siècle (1599), see Jones 1917, pp. 530–35 and 621, and Chaix, Dufour and Moeckli 1966, pp. 144, 152.
9 Besides omitting a digression on the execution of Mary, Queen of Scots, which the French generally deplored, the English text begins to diverge from Matthieu's on p. 216 and leaves it decisively behind on p. 219. I have not identified the French original that presumably lies behind the new material.
10 See King 2008, p. 27.
11 The spiritual charge of the metaphor is what enables Matthieu effectively to reliteralize it in *La Guisiade*. It also furnishes his lugubrious concluding note to Book 4 of the *Histoire des derniers troubles*, 1596 (fol. 250^r–51^r) – another omission, interestingly, from the translation.
12 This presumption matches the reasonable theory that, for political reasons, the Quarto texts (beginning with the First Quarto in 1600) omit the Prologue and choruses as originally performed. See, notably, Patterson 1989 on the 'representational instability' (p. 86) thereby imported into *H5*. Cf. Chapter 2, pp. 20–21, on the possible association of Guise with Essex.
13 The original of this pamphlet, *Excellent et libre discours, sur l'estat present de la France*, was included in another of Goulart's compilations, *Le troisiesme recveil* (1593).
14 Cf. my discussion in *Shakespeare, Marlowe and the Politics of France*, 2002, pp. 189–91.
15 It is instructive to trace, by way of the OED, the evolution of the term from its early seventeenth-century ecclesiastical origins. On the latter, see Kelley 1981, esp. pp. 244–51 and 276–97.
16 See esp. *Les guerriers de Dieu* (1990), *La nuit de la Saint-Barthélemy* (1994) and *La genèse de la Réforme française, 1520–1562*, 1996.
17 This is confirmed by Simonini 1952, p. 17. The closest thing to a systematic survey, with close analysis of language teaching methods, is by Kibbee 1991, esp. pp. 94–187. See also Yates 1968, pp. 139–73, and Lawrence 2005, *passim*.
18 See Deierkauf-Holsboer 1968, pp. 40–41, 44–45, 173–74, 176–77, and Baschet 1982, pp. 101–2 n.1.

2

On the generic cusp: *Richard II*, *La Guisiade* and the invention of tragic heroes

Early modern English tragedy is a richly unstable phenomenon not least in its variant approaches, by comparison to Senecan and French Humanist precedents, to an element that the genre imposes in some form: the tragic protagonist. I am far from taking for granted the mimetic model that may be read into the 'mature Shakespeare', which has tended to loom as a telos in critical retrospect. On the contrary, beginning with an approach to Othello by way of Samson and Holofernes in Chapter 4, and notably across discussions of Hamlet and Antony in *French Reflections*, I put a premium on the fragmentation, split-modelling and discontinuity to which Shakespeare's tragic protagonists are subjected: the deconstruction of mimetic illusion. Such effects depend, however, on the existence of the illusion in the first place, and it is widely agreed that in *Richard II* we may observe it in formation (if not necessarily in action). This process may be closely correlated with a precedent on the French side – one, moreover, that offers an intriguing perspective on the evolution from history play to tragedy within Shakespeare's œuvre and, more broadly, on the English dramatic scene during the 1590s, when French and English political issues were in especially close and dynamic conjunction.

I

It is irresistible to view the question of *Richard II*'s genre bifocally – that is, through the contrasting lenses of its original titles: in the early Quarto editions, beginning with the first of 1597, it is labelled *The Tragedie of King Richard the second*, while the First Folio of 1623 terms it *The life and death of King Richard the Second*. Too much should not be made of this double identity: the case is not unique – *King Lear* underwent a reverse renaming between first Quarto (1608) and Folio – while both 'history' and 'tragedy' often served as catch-all terms in the period. Then, the very organization of the Folio collection applied generic pressures: its 'Catalogue' naturally slots the play into a chronological niche as the second of the 'Histories', a category evidently redefined so that *King Lear* no longer has a place. There is no harm, however, in taking the double title as a cue to consider the shifting, if not competing, ideas of chronicle history and tragedy within *Richard II*; when we do so, it is Shakespeare's reconceptualization of the latter form that is thrown into relief, including the figure of the protagonist perversely bent on his own destruction.

Certainly, King Richard outgrows his political and moral functionality, his figural embodiment of faulty monarchy, as modelled on such predecessors as his namesake in *Woodstock*, Marlowe's Edward II, and Shakespeare's own Henry VI. He also traces a downward trajectory far more complex than the formula of free fall (at spiritual expense) prescribed by, say, Lydgate, and dutifully swallowed by the *Mirror for Magistrates* and, most immediately to the point, Samuel Daniel in *The Civil Wars* (1595). Richard is felt to take on both emotional weight and psychological depth – an impression produced by his relentlessly eloquent oscillation between flagrant self-deception and agonizing self-knowledge. The result is that the play's cold-blooded political morality, which attributes disaster to the king's errors and others' ability to exploit them, fails to efface the illusion of not only his flaws (the plural of that loaded term is surely to be preferred) but his sufferings as larger than life, indeed universal, and, most ironically, as transcending the banality to which he himself would reduce them for his own *Mirror for Magistrates* anthology: 'sad stories of the death of kings' (III.ii.155).

As history wends its course through the Second Tetralogy (itself a critical construct, but an intertextually mandated one), Richard's specifically political significance is bound to take posthumous precedence, and it becomes highly variable: when Hotspur self-servingly evokes 'that sweet lovely rose' (*1H4*, I.iii.175), he effectively confutes Juliet's claim that odours transcend language (*Rom.*, II.ii.43–44). But within Richard's own play, the figure of tragedy he becomes as he victimizes himself along with others, weaving himself into the web of words that he mistakes for the fabric of the universe, transcends the mechanisms of history to prefigure far-flung successors: Hamlet, Lear, Othello, Macbeth, Antony, Coriolanus.

Both because such characterization was once metonymic for critics of the supreme Shakespearean achievement, eliciting much neo-Aristotelian encomium, and because the debunking fashion of recent years has taken it as mere metaphysical mystification, we risk underestimating the technical innovation in English drama represented by Richard as tragic protagonist. The idea may, however, be making a comeback, to judge from Charles R. Forker's willingness, in the Introduction to his Arden edition, to (re)make front page news of the fact that, 'In the character of Richard, Shakespeare achieved a higher degree of psychological complexity than he had yet managed in tragedy.' Indeed, Forker comes close to putting Descartes before the early modern horse when he perceives a case study at once in political theory and neurotic practice:

> What is unique and fresh in *Richard II* is the stress on the divinity that was thought to hedge kings, the abandonment of historical diffusiveness and the probing not merely of divine right as a concept but of the unstable personality of a king who puts his whole trust in its theoretical protections. (Forker [ed.] 2001, p. 1)

New Historicists may rest assured that, even with regard to his mimeticism, I come to contextualize the tragic hero, not to celebrate him. In the absence of an established English context, however, I do so with reference to a French dramatic aberration: *La Guisiade* of Pierre Matthieu, a tragedy published in three editions in 1589 (and perhaps staged as well). I cannot prove Shakespeare's familiarity with *La Guisiade*, although it seems to me highly probable. It may simply be that the issue of a politically overweening but personally (and dynastically) self-destructive monarch with blood on his hands was in the political *air du temps* on both sides of the Channel. In any case, the generic doubleness of *Richard II* is strikingly, perhaps even uniquely, anticipated, in Matthieu's work, whose political lesson was, at the very moment of Shakespeare's staging, being played out on the tragic stage of French history.

II

Pierre Matthieu, a lawyer by training, was a militant in the Holy League in Lyons at the moment when Henri III's assassination at Blois of the Duke of Guise and his brother Cardinal Louis de Lorraine inspired him to hitch his proven play-writing skills to the revolutionary wagon. The result is aberrant in a literary sense because it adapts to very recent political events and propagandistic imperatives the restrained neo-Senecanism that was *de rigueur* in contemporary French tragedy, whose subjects were overwhelmingly (like those of Matthieu's several previous plays) classical and biblical. The neo-classical framework does not quite collapse under the strain but it visibly cracks. There is no on-stage action; all the speech consists of monologue or two-way dialogue; the style (including Choruses) is resolutely lofty – like *Richard II*'s. Nevertheless, the episodic approach to the last stages of Henri III's political struggle with Guise at least gives a liberal interpretation to the Unity of Time. Indeed, Matthieu concluded by promising a sequel (never written) that would deal with 'la mort de Louys de Lorraine Cardinal, et de l'emprisonnement des Princes, et autres Seigneurs, avec une continuation de l'histoire, et de tout ce qui s'est passé depuis la cruauté exercee sur les corps morts, jusques au trespas de la Royne mere [the death of Cardinal Louis de Lorraine and the imprisonment of the Princes and other lords, with a continuation of the history and all that happened from the cruel treatment of the dead bodies until the death of the Queen Mother].'[1] Matthieu was, in effect, orienting himself toward the principle of the chronicle play – as well as, incidentally, presaging his improbable future vocation as the dutiful historiographer of Henri IV.

La Guisiade's generic aberrance has sufficed to displace it to the margins of French literary history. And from those margins it signposts a further road that French neo-classical drama chose, for whatever complex reasons, not to follow: the portrait of Henri III is painted in vivid colours of eloquent self-delusion, festering jealousy, compensation through treacherous violence, and the consequent sufferings of conscience – in short, with a range and intensity of psychological process that stand out, for a specialist in English drama, as proto-Shakespearean. In this respect, too, the play sets itself apart from the sixteenth-century French mainstream, which rarely takes characterization beyond conventional declamatory postures.

Given my focus on the tragic protagonist, I do not dwell on the multiple points of contact between *La Guisiade* and contemporary English political discourse, dramatic and otherwise. That has been my preoccupation elsewhere.[2] But it remains to the point that Shakespeare's representation of English medieval history was predisposed intertextually to evoke the downfall of the Valois dynasty, hence the war of disputed succession in which English forces had served in 1591 (under Essex at Rouen), and as recently as 1594 (under John Norris in Brittany). The contemporary resonance had already been exploited by Marlowe in *Edward II*, when he chose for his only dramatic excursion into English history an analogous political disaster case – a figure who, thanks especially to the liaison with Gaveston, had himself been newly encoded in League propaganda as a type of Henri III, enthralled to his *mignon* Épernon.[3] (The latter is the prime villain of *La Guisiade*, where the parallel with Edward II is also mentioned explicitly.) In this context, Marlowe's portrayal of an unscrupulous strongman emerging to oppose an ineffectual monarch, and in unholy alliance with a foreign (indeed French) queen, might well have evoked the Duke of Guise and Catherine de Medici. Finally, there is very little distance between the boasts of Marlowe's Mortimer and of his Guise in *The Massacre at Paris*, even if the former will get his comeuppance in the next scene, the latter sixteen years hence:

>The prince I rule, the queen do I command,
>And with a lowly congé to the ground
>The proudest lords salute me as I pass;
>I seal, I cancel, I do what I will.
>Feared am I more than loved; let me be feared,
>And when I frown, make all the court look pale.
>>(*Edward II*, ed. Forker, 1994, V.iv.46–51)
>
>The Mother Queen works wonders for my sake
>And in my love entombs the hope of France.
>[...]
>As Caesar to his soldiers, so say I:
>Those that hate me will I learn to loathe.
>Give me a look that, when I bend the brows,
>Pale death may walk in furrows of my face.
>>(*Massacre*, ed. Oliver, 1968, ii.73–74, 95–98)

In fact, the 'couple' of Guise and Catherine were regularly on stage throughout the period in the perennially popular *Massacre*, whose first recorded performance in 1593 was seemingly followed by revivals in the following year, in 1598, and in November 1601.[4] And latterly, at least, the political situation in England might be supposed to have inflected reception in the direction of *Richard II*. The last revival of *Massacre* postdates by some months Essex's attempted *coup d'état* and, hence, the famous commissioned revival of Shakespeare's history that preceded it. Yet dramatic illustrations of ambitious strongmen challenging an enfeebled monarch would surely have been tinged, for audiences, by the increasingly tense English situation at least from 1598, when Essex insulted the queen, received the famous box on the ear, and put his hand menacingly on his sword. Certainly, the posthumous French analogue produced in 1602 by the treachery to Henri IV of Charles, Duke of Biron, was immediately applied to the case of Essex on both sides of the Channel, and in both French and English.

With regard to the *Massacre*, Elizabeth did not say (as far as we know), 'I am Henri III, know you not that?', but then Marlowe said it for her through the dying monarch's concern for his 'sister England', to whom he sends 'warning of her treacherous foes' (xxiv.50–51). The propaganda point there is religious – Pope Sixtus V's declaration of open season on heretic rulers – but the play actually presents the assassination primarily as an act of political revenge, aimed at 'Valois his line' (xxiii.7) by the surviving brother of a Machiavellian demagogue for whom religion was always a mere pretext. Essex's militant Protestantism would not necessarily have prevented an audience from associating him with Guise as a political force any more than it precluded his identification with Biron, likewise of ultra-Catholic profession. Indeed, in the semiotic practices of the period, superficial opposition may actually function to encourage the perception of structural resemblance.[5]

If *Richard II* does not come, like *Edward II*, with a ready-made set of symbolic connections with the political events dramatized in *La Guisiade* and *The Massacre at Paris*, Shakespeare's play does encourage its audience to think historically about English–French relations in ways that had contemporary implications. To this extent, it pursues the method of the First Tetralogy, in which the political ineffectuality and ostentatious religiosity of Henry VI, under whom French–English wars gave way to English civil ones, might likewise have evoked Henri III, though hardly as a figure of psychological complexity or tragic depth. In *Richard II*, the king's French marriage provides a notable occasion, as mediated in part by the sympathetic treatments of Richard by medieval French commentators, for evoking his reign (not without distortion) as a brief interval of cross-Channel harmony within the Hundred Years War.

English–French national issues and sentiments are also aggressively present in the anonymous *Woodstock* – in terms, remarkably, that invert contemporary League discourse. *Woodstock* is unique among Elizabethan treatments of the reign of Richard – dramatic, poetic (*The Civile Wars*), or historical – for its unequivocal Lancastrianism: the play's Richard ('of Bordeaux', as he is repeatedly termed) is a Frenchified, minion-muddled hedonist; Woodstock ('Plain Thomas'), who – according to the chronicles – was as unscrupulous and ambitious as they come, is made to stand for wholesome Englishness and the welfare of the common people. This mirrors the League's crude denigration of Henri III – accused, as in *La Guisiade*, of Anglophilia (besides even more lurid vices) – and its elevation of Guise into an emblem of pure Frenchness. The climax of both plays is the royally ordered murder of the people's champions. Even the symbolism of Calais comes into both as a measure of royal ingratitude: the town was gained by Woodstock and his brothers for the English crown (Rossiter [ed.] 1946, V.i.158 ff.), only to serve as the setting for his murder; its recovery by the heroic François de Guise, father of the present Duke, is prominent among that family's patriotic exploits, as celebrated by Matthieu (*La Guisiade*, ed. Lobbes, 1990, l. 93).

Also corresponding is the retribution anticipated – the pursuit of justice by family and followers, the murderer's sense of guilt. But this last parallel points up a significant divergence, one which returns me to *Richard II*, and to characterization. *Woodstock* may assign Richard a Cain-like impulse to hide from God, along with the terrible knowledge that to do so is impossible, but the reaction is imposed by circumstances; the king suffers a drastic downturn in his fortunes and intuits worse – with reason, in the long term, although the play stops well short of his eventual deposition and death:[6]

> ... the fearful wrath of heaven
> Sits heavy on our heads for Woodstock's death.
> Blood cries for blood; and that almighty hand
> Permits not murder unrevenged to stand.
> Come, come, we yet may hide ourselves from worldly strength,
> But Heaven will find us out, and strike at length.
> (*Woodstock*, ed. Rossiter, 1946, V.iv.47–52)

By contrast, *La Guisiade*, through the curse of Guise's mother (Madame de Nemours), raises Cain in Henri's character, so to speak, by conjuring for him a gnawing anguish worthy of Macbeth, haunted banquet and all:

> ... mon Dieu justicier ne lairra impunie
> Ta fiere crualté, ta blesme tyrannie:
> Comme un second Cain, tu auras à tes pas
> L'ombre de mon enfant, en prenant ton repas,
> Le sang de ce grand Duc fera bouffir tes veines,
> Tu seras escorché, et mis entre les geines
> D'un renaissant remord, les Panniques terreurs
> Combleront ton cerveau de craintes et d'horreurs,
> Et te mussant couard en un fort, la vengeance
> Ira tousjours sommer ta pasle conscience.
> On te verra contraint du remort qui te point,
> Crier mercy au peuple, ayant la torche au poing.
>
> [... my God, dispenser of justice, will not fail
> Your fury, your livid tyranny, to assail:
> Like a second Cain, you shall be dogged at your heels
> By the ghost of my child, as you sit at your meals;
> The blood of that noble Duke shall swell up your veins;
> You shall be flayed alive, put to the utmost pains
> Of relentless remorse; panic-terrors your head
> Shall fill to overflowing with horror and dread –
> And if, though a coward, you feign yourself undaunted,
> Your pale conscience shall ever by vengeance be haunted.
> The pricking of remorse will drive you forth to stand
> And beg pardon of the people with torch in hand.]
> (ed. Lobbes, 1990, ll. 2143–54)

Such inward punishment figures tragic anagnorisis, as quintessentially realized by Shakespeare's Richard: 'I wasted time, and now doth time waste me' (V.v.49).

On the generic cusp 23

Even in thus approaching *La Guisiade* more closely than does *Woodstock*, however, *Richard II* parts company with it. Indeed, the intertextual relation provocatively bifurcates in the directions, precisely, of history and tragedy. For the blood guilt of Shakespeare's king is in the past, and to the (considerable) extent that Bullingbrook renews it, the story resembles Matthieu's prophecy (and history's reality) of merited retribution visited upon a royal murderer: at this level, *Richard II* shadows forth the sequel of *La Guisiade*, as it openly stages that of *Woodstock*. At the same time, the punishment of Richard hardly puts paid to history's bloody debt; it ensures the perpetuation of the cycle of violent retribution, as, in reality, the killing of Henri III unleashed a new round of civil wars in France. That is the future tragedy, not of Richard, but of Bullingbrook and the House of Lancaster, and it is therefore fitting that the curse of Cain evoked by Madame de Nemours should be transferred to him along with the 'care' of kingship previously bestowed by Richard. The transfer is manifested when the new king himself finally falls from historical signifier into tragic subjectivity through his futile projection of responsibility upon Exton:

> The guilt of conscience take thee for thy labor,
> But neither my good word nor princely favor.
> With Cain go wander thorough shades of night,
> And never show thy head by day nor light.
> Lords, I protest my soul is full of woe
> That blood should sprinkle me to make me grow.
>   (V.vi.41–46)

Meanwhile Richard II's acutely present and personal tragedy is shunted onto another intertextual track. Between his deposition and his death, the character largely recuperates – guilty though he remains – Guise's role as victim and martyr, complete with Christ-like trappings. Richard's invocations of Judas and Pilate, beginning on his return from Ireland (III.ii.132–34) and culminating in the deposition scene, help put the parallel in place, although self-dramatization cushions their impact. What seals it, however, is the sequence leading to his death initiated with his desire to 'go'; when Bullingbrook asks, 'Whither?', he replies, 'Whither you will, so I were from your sights' (IV.i.314–15). The evocation of the Gospel of John here, while not widely noted, exerts particular textual force precisely because Richard does not self-consciously impose it: 'Simon Peter said unto him, Lord, whither goest thou? Jesus answered him, Whither I go, thou canst not follow me now: but thou shalt follow me afterwards' (John 13:36); 'But now I go my way to him that sent me, and none of you asketh me, Whither goest thou? But because I have said these things unto you, your hearts are full of sorrow' (16:5–6). 'Whither goest thou?' is likewise intoned in *La Guisiade*, as the Duke sets out on his final journey ('Où vas tu?' [ed. Lobbes, 1990, l. 1880], 'Où allez vous?' [l. 2050]).

In Shakespeare there follow Richard's pathetic last moments: the parting from his queen, the tormented soliloquy, the account of his horse's pride at bearing Bullingbrook – the latter glancing at the same pride that Guise disclaims in his final soliloquy and that God never fails to punish, that of 'Le superbe qui veut contre un Roy entreprendre [That man of haughty pride who would usurp a king]' (l. 1868). Richard's valorous struggle against his murderers, which resembles Guise's, is in the chronicles; there, however, he is struck down before he can speak. Here he gets to draw the same moral about the crime of shedding his blood as is expressed by Matthieu's Messenger, for whom the blood of Guise 'ses meurtriers devant son Dieu appelle [shall his murderers to God deliver]' (ed. Lobbes, 1990, l. 2070), and to complete the parallel with analogous pious last words: 'Mount, mount, my soul! thy seat is up on high, / Whilst my gross flesh sinks downward, here to die' (V.v.111–12).[7]

Paradoxically, an element that Shakespeare chose not to incorporate from one of his putative sources tends to confirm that, for other Elizabethans as well, recent events in France coloured the English revolution of 1400. Daniel's *The Civile Wars* is widely suspected of having encouraged Shakespeare's development of Richard as a tragic figure, contributing particularly the king's sorrowful encounter with his Queen. Also of interest, however (if hardly for its poetical quality), is the summary of the political moral:

> And thus one king most nere in blood allide
> Is made th'oblation for the others peace:
> Now onely one, both name and all beside
> Intirely hath, plurality doth cease....
> And henceforth he is absolutely king,
> No crownes but one, this deed confirms the thing.
> (Bk. III, Stanza 85 [Bullough (ed.), 1957–75, 3: 460])

This language, unprecedented in the chronicles, is very close to that widely attributed to Henri III with respect to the Guisean threat. It is resoundingly deployed in *La Guisiade* both when the king resolves on his murder and at the moment of its accomplishment:

> Je regneray tout seul ainsi que mes ayeux.
> On ne peut diviser la Monarchie à deux.
> Cest unique pouvoir en mesme temps n'assemble
> Deux Princes compagnons pour commander ensemble....
> Je veux seul estre Roy, je ne veux desormais
> Avoir pour compagnon un Prince trouble-paix.

> [I shall reign alone as my ancestors have done.
> Kingship cannot be cut into two: it is one –
> A sole and singular power, which cannot bring
> Together princely partners to make a joint king. . . .
> I want to be king alone; I want, from now on,
> To have no trouble-making prince as my companion.]
> (ed. Lobbes, 1990, ll. 1683–92)

> Il s'escrie, Tout seul, tout seul regner je veux:
> Je suis Roy maintenant, nous ne sommes plus deux.

> [He cried, 'All alone, all alone I wish to reign.
> I am the king henceforth; we are no longer twain.']
> (ed. Lobbes, 1990, ll. 2083–84)

These are lines that would well have suited Shakespeare's king, had the affair between him and Bullingbrook gone the other way.

III

I now refocus the discussion on the predeposition career of Shakespeare's Richard, those specifically delusional aspects of his mismanagement of royal power which affiliate him, not with the hero of *La Guisiade*, but with its villain, and thereby set up his belated self-realization. The mismanagement itself takes broadly parallel forms, in keeping with similar historical 'data': the vices that both Bullingbrook and Guise propose to cure include the indulgence of minions, abusive taxation, and consorting with the enemy – the French in the former case, the English in the latter. Both monarchs, more fundamentally, have offended against God – Richard by his murder of Gloucester, Henri by his sympathetic toleration of heretics. What uniquely lends Shakespeare's Richard his resemblance to the French king, however, is his secret knowledge of his own moral unfitness – knowledge that both monarchs attempt to dispel through eloquence (power over words in the place of real power) and by taking refuge in their status as the Lord's anointeds.

On the latter point Shakespeare's Richard goes well beyond all precursors – except Matthieu's Henri:

> Not all the water in the rough rude sea
> Can wash the balm off from an anointed king;
> The breath of worldly men cannot depose
> The deputy elected by the Lord.
> For every man that Bullingbrook hath press'd
> To lift shrewd steel against our golden crown,

> God for his Richard hath in heavenly pay
> A glorious angel; then if angels fight,
> Weak men must fall, for heaven still guards the right.
> (III.ii.54–62)

> Je suis l'Oinct du Seigneur, je suis Roy grand et fort,
> Je suis sur les François juge en dernier ressort,
> Ma poictrine et mon dos, comme d'une cuirass,
> S'arme de mon bon droict, j'ai l'amour en la face,
> J'ay en main le pouvoir, et le courage au cueur,
> Asseurez instruments pour me rendre vainqueur:
> L'inexpugnable escu qui mon bras environne,
> Est la droicte equité, qui ne cognoit personne,
> Et pour lance cruelle, ô mutins, contre vous
> J'ay le commandement qui vous estonne tous.

> [I am a great and potent king, the Lord's anointed,
> As judge of last resort over the French appointed;
> My breast and my back, as if clad in armour plates,
> My true right protects; from my face love radiates;
> I have courage in my heart, and in my hand power,
> Sure means to bring about my victorious hour.
> The impervious shield that my arm boldly wears
> Is blind equity itself, which no person spares.
> And as my cruel lance, aimed at your mutiny,
> I wield what will amaze you: stark authority.]
> (ed. Lobbes, 1990, ll. 505–14)

As the playwright not only lavishly illustrates but points up in glossing commentaries provided for the third edition of the tragedy,[8] Matthieu's king, like Shakespeare's, thrives on public ceremonial and proves a master – that is to say, a victim – of self-dramatization, talking himself into elemental omnipotence: 'Si le peuple me fuit, le ciel me favorise [Heaven will stay with me, if every subject flies]' (ed. Lobbes, 1990, l. 399). Thus, too, he claims (apostrophizing France as Richard does his 'Dear earth . . .' [III.ii.6 ff.]) that at his return from Poland, 'Je vis tes ennemies s'enfuir à mon ombre, / Comme aux rais du soleil se cache la nuict sombre [I saw your foes flee when I loomed on the horizon, / As night skulks off to hide from the rays of the sun]' (ll. 491–92). So Richard, returned from Ireland, fantasizes that his sun-like rising will make 'murthers, treasons, and detested sins, / The cloak of night being pluck'd from off their backs, / Stand bare and naked, trembling at themselves' (III.ii.44–46).

The rhetorical balloons are pricked in both cases by blunt counsel – from Catherine de Médicis, from York:

> ... j'ay peur que si vous n'appaisez
> Tant de cueurs contre vous justement embrasez,
> Que regnerez tout seul, et n'aura personne,
> Sinon quelque Mignon, qui serve la Couronne.
>
> [... I fear that you will scarcely thus assuage
> So many hearts inflamed against you with just rage,
> That you will reign alone, with no man's good opinion
> And no one left to serve the crown, except some minion.]
> (ed. Lobbes, 1990, ll. 437–40)
>
> You pluck a thousand dangers on your head,
> You lose a thousand well-disposed hearts,
> And prick my tender patience to those thoughts
> Which honor and allegiance cannot think.
> (II.i.205–8)

But the inflated royal rhetoric is also self-undercutting, predisposed to be redeployed for extremities of despair, the embracing of victimization. Both Richard and Henri imagine themselves thrust out of power into a 'hermitage' (III.ii.148) – 'quelque cloistre [some monastery]' (ed. Lobbes, 1990, l. 428), as indeed the League sometimes envisaged for Henri. It is a small step to imagining himself consigned to 'A little little grave' (III.iii.154). So does Henri, too, effectively, in conversation with the mysteriously named 'N.N.', the personification at once of his secret fears, his Machiavellian counsellors, and the voice of diabolical suggestion: 'Guise veut / Vous tuer pour regner, si vaincre il ne vous peut [Guise is willing, / If he cannot prevail, to take your crown by killing]' (ll. 1663–64).

IV

Such discovery of the fragility and vulnerability of a previously impervious self-image is central to the production of tragic subjectivity in Shakespeare's protagonists. In *Richard II*, that trajectory is driven, from start to finish, by a jealousy inextricably blending the personal and the political. It is telling that Richard's final moments are introduced by his outburst against the horse Barbary for proudly bearing Bullingbrook on his coronation day – an outburst that recoils, typically, against himself:

> Forgiveness, horse! why do I rail on thee,
> Since thou, created to be aw'd by man,
> Wast born to bear? I was not made a horse,
> And yet I bear a burthen like an ass,
> Spurr'd, gall'd, and tir'd by jauncing Bullingbrook.
> (V.v.90–94)

Jealousy is likewise the mainspring of Henri's political reactions throughout *La Guisiade* – indeed, the keynote announced in the first words of Matthieu's introductory 'Discours'. That jealousy, moreover, is explicitly allowed to colour, and implicitly to impair, the claim to inalienable divine right in which he takes refuge when he confronts the notion of sharing the kingship:

> Mon cueur enjalouzé ne le permettra pas.
> Un Roy est toujours Roy, mesme apres son trespas:
> On ne peut effacer le Royal caractere,
> Que Dieu grave du doigt en une ame hommagere.
>
> [My heart, filled with jealousy, will never agree;
> A king is a king – in life, for eternity.
> One can't wipe from the soul the royal character,
> When God has pleased with his finger to carve it there.]
> (ed. Lobbes, 1990, ll. 1687–90)

'N.N.' tempts Henri into murderous action by harping on his rival's popularity: 'Il a gaigné le cueur du people et de l'Eglise: / On leve le chapeau quand on parle de Guise [The hearts of the people and the Church he can claim: / They all take off their hats when they mention his name]' (ed. Lobbes, 1990, ll. 1669–70). An alert English reader might have recalled Holinshed's account of Bullingbrook's passage into exile:

> A woonder it was to see what number of people ran after him in everie towne and street where he came, before he took the sea, lamenting and bewailing his departure, as who would saie, that when he departed, the onelie shield, defense, and comfort of the commonwealth was vaded and gone.[9]

Yet the chronicles remain silent on the king's reaction to Bullingbrook's popularity. It is Shakespeare who gives Richard a bitter and contemptuous effusion in the manner of Matthieu's Henri, who likewise conflates personal injury with political danger, on the false humility of 'high Herford' (I.iv.2):

> Ourself and Bushy, Bagot here and Green,
> Observ'd his courtship to the common people,
> How he did seem to dive into their hearts
> With humble and familiar courtesy,
> What reverence he did throw away on slaves,
> Wooing poor craftsmen with the craft of smiles
> And patient underbearing of his fortune,
> As 'twere to banish their affects with him.
> Off goes his bonnet to an oyster-wench,
> A brace of draymen bid God speed him well,
> And had the tribute of his supple knee,

> With 'Thanks, my countrymen, my loving friends',
> As were our England in reversion his,
> And he our subjects' next degree in hope.
>
> (23–36)

It is striking that, from his subsequent analytic perspective in the *Histoire des derniers troubles*, Matthieu came to view Guise's calculating cultivation of popular favour with much the same eye: 'Le Duc de Guise pour commander aux grans, s'assubjectissoit aux moindre d'vn bout de rüe à l'autre, il passoit le bonnet au poing, salüant ou de la teste, ou de la main, ou de la parole, iusques aux plus petits crocheteurs [The Duke of Guise, that he might give commands to the great, rendered himself subject to the least from one end of the street to the other; he passed by with his hat in his hand, proffering a greeting with his head, with his hand, or with speech, even to the most lowly porters]' (1596, fol. 242ʳ).

Shakespeare's scene looks forward to Richard's sarcasm at the expense of Bullingbrook's 'supple knee' when his rival's popularity yields the concrete political results he had helplessly anticipated:

> Fair cousin, you debase your princely knee
> To make the base earth proud with kissing it.
> Me rather had my heart might feel your love
> Than my unpleased eye see your courtesy.
> Up, cousin, up, your heart is up, I know,
> Thus high at least [*touching his crown*], although
>   your knee be low.
>
> (III.iii.190–95)

Here it is especially instructive to compare Marlowe's *Massacre*, where Shakespeare might also have found a model involving Henri III and Guise – one also conceivably produced, as I have proposed, by a rewriting of *La Guisiade*.[10] The sarcasm of Marlowe's Henry, however, issues from and returns to forthright anger:

> Guise, wear our crown, and be thou King of France
> And as dictator make or war or peace
> Whilst I cry *placet* like a senator!
> I cannot brook thy haughty insolence. . . .
>
> (ed. Oliver, 1968, xix.55–58)

Marlowe's villain rather vaguely traces the contours of his historical model, who returned to Paris, Bullingbrook-like, in blatant defiance of royal authority and to popular acclaim that drove the king into humiliating retreat (on

12 May 1588, the so-called Day of the Barricades). The emphasis is on his demagogic Caesarism, which provokes Henry to assess and counteract a real political threat: 'Did they of Paris entertain him so? / Then means he present treason to our state' (xix.75). Only an overweening arrogance could blind this Guise to the glaring *double entendre* with which this Henry deliberately assures, and lures, him:

> Cousin, assure you I am resolute –
> Whatsoever any whisper in mine ears[11] –
> Not to suspect disloyalty in thee:
> And so, sweet coz, farewell.
> (ed. Oliver, 1968, xxi.44–47)

La Guisiade, by contrast, anticipates Shakespeare by tracing the royal resentment, tinged with paranoia ('Chacun dit', 'L'on me dit tous les jours'), to the root of impotence:

> Et bien que dictes-vous, mon cousin? Vous avez
> Plus de feux allumez qu'assoupir n'en pouvez,
> Chacun dit que ce feu se nourrit de la flamme
> De quelque ambition, qui brasille en vostre ame:
> L'on me dit tous les jours qu'en me faussant la foy
> Vous liguez mes subjects de nouveau contre moy.
>
> [So, then, Cousin, what have you got to say? The fires
> You've kindled may spread beyond even your desires.
> Everyone says that the blaze is fed by a flame,
> Burning in your soul, that deserves ambition's name;
> They tell me that, breaking your oath of loyalty,
> You form leagues, day by day, of subjects against me.]
> (ed. Lobbes, 1990, ll. 549–54)

Such feelings of inadequacy cannot dissemble straightforwardly, as it were; the words that lead Matthieu's noble and trusting Guise to his destruction are twisted grotesquely out of their true meaning precisely because they express what Henri, despite himself, knows to be true:

> ... mon bon Cousin, Hé Dieu! qui est celuy
> Que j'ayme mieux que vous? Non, je ne voy personne
> Qui ayme plus que vous l'honneur de la coronne.
>
> [... Good Cousin, for God's sake, who is more dear
> To me than you? I could turn the world upside-down
> And find none who loves more the honour of the crown.]
> (ed. Lobbes, 1990, ll. 1830–32)

The self-pity enfolded in such scathing irony, with its gesture towards the gulf between words and actions in which the king himself is lost, is profoundly Riccardian. It comes remarkably close to making the villain of Matthieu's piece, whom League propagandists were generally content to dismiss as an inhuman monster, into a highly plausible human one in the 'mature' Shakespearean tragic mould. But then, on the other side of the Channel the English call their own, that mould had yet to be moulded.

Notes

1 *La Guisiade*, ed. Lobbes, 1990, p. 166 ('Advertissement au Lecteurs sur la continuation de ceste Tragedie'); trans. Hillman 2005, p. 269. I cite my published translation throughout, whose line numbering, in the case of verse, corresponds to that of Lobbes's edition.
2 See *Shakespeare, Marlowe and the Politics of France*, 2002, pp. 84–97, 105–9, *et passim*.
3 See *Shakespeare, Marlowe and the Politics of France*, 2002, pp. 97–104.
4 See Oliver (ed.), Introduction, *The Massacre at Paris*, 1968, pp. xlix–l; references are to scene and line numbers.
5 See my discussion of this mechanism in 'The Tragic Channel-Crossings of George Chapman, Part I', 2004, esp. p. 34.
6 Although the manuscript is incomplete, it appears to lack only a single sheet (Rossiter [ed.] 1946, n. to V.vi.34–35).
7 Cf. Guise's last words according to Matthieu:

> Est-ce pour mes pechez? Dieu pens pitié de moy;
> Je t'ay bien offencé, mais j'ay la conscience
> Au devoir vers mon Roy luisante d'innocence.
> Reçois mon ame ô Dieu! . . .
>
> [Is it for my sins? Then I pray God may have mercy!
> True, I have greatly offended You, but my conscience
> Concerning king and duty shines with innocence.
> Receive my soul, O God! . . .]
> (*La Guisiade*, ed. Lobbes, 1990, ll. 2072–75)

8   Cependant les Estats se commencent avec un autant heureux principe, que la fin en fut malheureuse. Le Roy commença son harangue d'un stil tant orné, et avec telle emphase qu'il semblait vouloir seul emporter la palme d'eloquence.

[Nevertheless, the Estates got underway as auspiciously as they ended unhappily. The King began his speech in such a finely crafted style, and with such delivery, that he seemed to desire the prize for eloquence exclusively for himself.] ('Discours sur le sujet de ceste Tragedie', ed. Lobbes, 1990, pp. 66–67; trans. Hillman, 2005, p. 178)

Le Roy entra en la salle ayant son grand Ordre au col, toute l'assemblee se tenant debout à teste descouverte jusques à ce que luy, et les Roynes estant assises, il prononça son harangue, tout le suject de laquelle le Poëte a reduit icy, non avec l'eloquence ny la grace dont elle fut pronouncee.

[The King entered the hall wearing his great Order around his neck, the whole assembly standing with heads uncovered until, he and the queens having been seated, he pronounced his speech, of which the poet has given a reduced version, which, however, has neither the eloquence nor the grace with which it was delivered.] ('Argument' [Scène 2a], ed. Lobbes, 1990, p. 118; trans. Hillman, 2005, pp. 221–22)

9 Cited in Bullough (ed.) 1957–75, 3: 394.
10 See *Shakespeare, Marlowe and the Politics of France*, 2002, pp. 84–97.
11 Especially given Marlowe's recuperation of Épernon ('Epernoun') as a counsellor of his king, this line gestures ironically towards diabolical portrayals of that minion in League visual propaganda; in specific relation to Matthieu's play, intertextually undercut is the similar representation of 'N.N.'

3

Out of their classical depth: from pathos to bathos in early English tragedy; or, the comedy of terrors

We tend to take for granted the creaky neo-Senecan machinery of the ghostly framing device in Kyd's *The Spanish Tragedy*, if not to snigger at its naïveté, as Beaumont found it easy to do in *The Knight of the Burning Pestle*: 'When I was mortal, this my costive corpse / Did lap up figs and raisins in the Strand ...' (V.290–1).[1] I propose here to listen attentively to those creaks and to some of their French-accented reverberations through English tragedy from the late 1580s on. *The Spanish Tragedy* serves as a natural starting point because the on-stage presence of Don Andrea and his companion Revenge bears material witness to a major structural dislocation, whereby a pagan eschatology is superimposed upon a play-world that is nominally Christian.

That eschatology, I think, is not just classically kitschy decor; its very kitschiness is functional. So it is more clearly in, say, *Antonio's Revenge* ten years later, where a mannerist Marston evokes 'Tragoedia Cothernata' (II.ii.220) by way of obtrusive Senecan scraps and grotesque postures – witness Andrugio's Ghost: 'I taste the joys of heaven / Viewing my son triumph in his black blood' (V.iii.67–68). At such moments, encouraged by our sense of the boy-actors who played the roles, we can, with reasonable confidence, affix the label of parody. By comparison, the pagan trappings of *The Spanish Tragedy* seem to take themselves seriously, as if claiming to delineate a valid and coherent metaphysics. It is in this sustained cause that they protest too much and, whether or not the pagans themselves took such fictions seriously – Seneca himself, in fact, pronounced them to be childish[2] – the cause is by definition a lost one for an Elizabethan audience.

Not only is the pagan eschatological framework of *The Spanish Tragedy* richly detailed – Andrea's narrative account of Hades impressively confines in little room the mighty underworld descents of epic – but it gets the first and last words, and very extravagant ones they are. Its paganism also obtrudes regularly into the main action, notably by way of Hieronimo – from his multiply plagiarized Latin fantasia on suicide (II.v.67 ff.), to the Senecan tags he opposes to the Bible's *'Vindicta mihi!'* (III.xiii.1 ff.), to his resolve to 'Knock at the dismal gates of Pluto's court' (III.xiii.110), itself echoed by Isabella's 'sorrow and despair', which 'hath cited me / To hear Horatio plead with Rhadamanth' (IV.ii.27–28). It is, of course, Hieronimo's decision to take the infernal work in hand that spectacularly prevails, and his infringement on the divine monopoly of revenge might have been expected to guarantee his damnation. Instead, it surprisingly engages the pagan machinery on his behalf: Andrea's ghost will personally 'lead Hieronimo where Orpheus plays, / Adding sweet pleasure to eternal days' (IV.v.23–24), while his request that 'sweet Revenge' (29) put his slain enemies in the place of mythology's archetypal sufferers – Tityus, Ixion, Sisyphus (31, 33, 40) – meets with eager assent:

> Then haste we down to meet thy friends and foes,
> To place thy friends in ease, the rest in woes:
> For here though death hath end their misery,
> I'll there begin their endless tragedy.
>
> (45–48)

Thus pagan eternity eclipses the Christian version – except that the glow of truth shines just brightly enough to build in the reminder that this hell is indeed a stage fable, standing in to some unknowable extent for one that is not. Balthazar will be left 'Repining at our joys that are above' (38); Pedringano will 'live, dying still in endless flames, / Blaspheming gods and all their holy names (43–44). The audience receives a parting kick in its willing suspension of disbelief.

Literal belief in this fabulous hell is never in question, and we are accordingly free to laugh away its excesses, rhetorical and otherwise, as sheer literary inventions. But the laughter will be uneasy, precisely in proportion as classical fable is felt to shadow Christian truth. I think that this uneasiness and uncertainty would attach to theatrical ghosts throughout the period, however vaguely or outrageously Senecan, even if, as Greenblatt insists in *Hamlet in Purgatory* (2001, esp. pp. 236–54), Hamlet's father stands out as a purgatorial tease (at once declaring and withholding the horrible 'secrets of my prison-house' and even using the word 'purg'd' [*Ham.*, I.v.13–14]). Even in his ultra-serious case, a nervous humour hovers in the air: 'Alas, poor ghost!' (4). I would further extend this theatrical phenomenon to those early tragic protagonists whose grotesque excesses in both suffering and cruelty blur the distinction between serious and comic in dramatic universes nominally homogeneous, whether pagan or Christian. An Elizabethan audience is regularly cued to respond with something like the mixed belief and disbelief structurally imposed in *The Spanish Tragedy*. Thus, in the thoroughly pagan *Titus Andronicus*, Aaron imports a nagging Christian diabolism, while in the

Christian-dominated *The Jew of Malta*, where religion is nevertheless up for grabs, Barabas' destiny as a human tea-bag assimilates damnation to pagan 'endless tragedy' by seemingly bringing imagined underworld horror concretely, but also farcically, *up* to earth.[3]

Such mixed effects stem, ultimately, from a sign defiantly declaring its own disjunction from its signified, the deferral of meaning through the intervention of signification. A classicized eternity can never *be* the 'promis'd end' of the Christian promise (or threat) but rather is doomed to remain the 'image of that horror' (*Lr.*, V.iii.264, 265) – a point self-reflexively made, in fact, by this exchange between the pagan Kent and Edgar. That unified medieval symbolic system that called a spade a spade, a devil a devil, is essentially disrupted. Self-conscious representation changes the equation, humour included, by making the whole indeterminately greater, because it is infinitely less than the sum of its parts. Of course, there was plenty of humour in the medieval stage imag(in)ings of that horror, which purported to be not images at all but incarnations in action of 'the thing itself' (*Lr.*, III.iv.106). The Last Judgement pageants abound in gleeful demonic recitals of sins committed and endless punishments in store; the Wakefield version is typical: 'Now shall they have rom in pik and tar ever dwelland; / Of thare sorow no some, bot ay to be yelland / In oure fostré' (*Medieval Drama*, ed. Bevington, 1975, ll. 597–99). But, as a function of the divine comedy, to which the comic devils are in service, these are not endless *tragedies* in any pertinent sense of that term, and among the 'warid wights' divided from the 'chosen childer' (ll. 528, 524), there is neither jesting nor cursing, but only the sorrowful echoing of the veritable Rhadamanth's awful Word:

> Alas, for doyll this day!
> Alas, that ever I it abode!
> Now am I dempned for ay;
> This dome may I not avoide.
>
> (ll. 512–15)

As for those comic caricatures of worldly tyranny often labelled theatrical ancestors of Barabas, the joke is naturally, supernaturally, and metadramatically, on them, as, in contrast to *The Spanish Tragedy*, the ending of false revels reveals true ones – witness Diabolus in the N. Town *Death of Herod*:

> This catel is min[e].
> I shall hem bring onto my celle.
> I shall hem teche pleys fin[e]
> And shewe such mirthe as is in helle.
>   (*Medieval Drama*, ed. Bevington, 1975, ll. 233–36)

If they acknowledge their endless ends at all, it is, like the Wakefield Cain, by ventriloquizing the moral:

> Now faire well, felows all, for I must nedys weynd,
> And to the dwill be thrall, warld withoutten end.
> Ordand there is my stall, with Sathanas the feynd.
> (*The Killing of Abel, Medieval Drama*, ed. Bevington, 1975, ll. 464–66)

They may retain a touch of the bullying blindness that damned them. Cain can still manage to curse, 'Ever ill might him befall that theder me commend' (l. 466), but none goes out with boisterous defiance like Barabas ('Die, life; fly, soul; tongue, curse thy fill and die!' [V.v.88]) or Richard III ('let us to it pell-mell; / If not to heaven, then hand in hand to hell' [*R3*, V.iii.312–13]) or, for that matter, Macbeth: 'Blow wind, come wrack, / At least we'll die with harness on our back' (*Mac.*, V.v.50–51). In dramatic universes that multiply replace medieval certainties with more or less fantastic 'dreams' figuring 'the dread of something after death' (*Ham.*, III.i.65, 77), such bluster is not comically absurd, like that of Herod, for whom Death and devils visibly wait in the background; it *un*-Herods Herod by taking on the thrilling charge of eschatological risk (the one most of us run). It is only a small step to rendering that risk explicit through conscious unknowing, the abyss that gapes uncannily for the lost souls of *The Duchess of Malfi*; Julia may serve as spokeswoman: 'I go, / I know not whither' (V.ii.288–89).

In terms of literary history, the master narrative here is the invention of English tragedy by grafting medieval traditions of representing comic evil onto re-'discovered' classical stock, particularly the models of Seneca, which supply the revenge motif and the proliferation of horrors. It is not surprising that such mixed breeding should branch off in incongruous metaphysical directions. But I also want to suggest that this hybrid, which flowers so abundantly and variously in the English theatrical climate from around 1585, is substantially a transplant, and that its origins shed light on the cultural work it continues to perform in its new soil.

In adapting this potted metaphor, I am conscious of trying to coax new life into a wilted perennial; as early as 1911, Elizabeth Jelliffe Macintire opined in *PMLA* (1911) that 'English classicism', which 'made firm roots in Elizabethan soil', was an 'exotic' plant that 'came of French stock' (p. 496). But her idea of what that meant was rather restrictive:

> The French mind tends to orderliness of idea and rule of procedure. It is the land of *convenance*. Hence, it is not strange that the notion of developing literature on some definite and well-conceived plan appears early in France.
> (Macintire 1911, p. 498)

From pathos to bathos in early English tragedy 37

Quaint as the expression now seems, the prejudice is still built into official literary history and, with respect to drama, it continues to exercise much the same influence as it did on Macintire, whose discussion of dramatic literature does not extend to the theatre. The French contribution remains firmly circumscribed within what used to be conceived as the Sidney-Pembroke sphere of influence, decorously extending from Philip Sidney himself, who set out the rules in *An Apology for Poetry*, to Fulke Greville's closet drama, to the Countess of Pembroke's translation of Robert Garnier's *Marc Antoine* and, more or less finally, to Samuel Daniel, with his unstaged *Cleopatra* and *Philotas*. This is the compact garden planted by Macintire (pp. 523–24), and subsequent criticism, by and large, has kept it carefully tended and free from weeds, on the assumption that flowers and weeds are different species. That assumption deserves to be delved to the root, and I do so here, not merely by extending French neo-classical influence to the Elizabethan theatre in its most public and popular form, but by declassicizing, with due caution, French drama itself. Such groundwork and replanting bears further fruit when I focus on various Antonies and Cleopatras in *French Reflections* (Chapter 3: 'Nursing Serpents: French Ripples within and beyond the "Pembroke Circle"').

I

There is no question but that the Italians and the French were first off the neo-Senecan mark, putting in place the generic scaffolding that enabled Sidney to praise *Gorboduc* (1561) as a trailblazer, although more for its poetry 'rising to the height of Seneca's style' than for its faulty 'circumstances' (Sidney, p. 134). It is striking that Sidney, writing about thirty years later, could find no more recent example of English neo-classical tragedy to praise, despite the appearance in the interim of translations of Seneca's plays, while the corpus of original works in Italy and, especially, France was already considerable. The Italian avatars, beginning with Cinthio's *Orbecce* (1544), are an obvious source of extravagant and sensationalistic horror.[4] What the French ones, especially those of Garnier, most obviously contribute is serious political thought with immediate, if cautious, applicability, given the profuse bleeding of the body politic from those 'wounds of civil war' whose very thought was painful to the English.[5] The apparatus of classical mythology, including the omnipresent motif of vengeance, is justified by classical historical settings but becomes a way of figuring the self-immolation of France through a concept that English scholars are likely to think of reflexively as quintessentially Marlovian: the scourge of God. Diabolical forces of division are unleashed upon a nation that has abused the divine favour, with the implicit promise that, once due humility, piety and virtue are restored, the incendiaries of discord will be consumed in the flame of God's righteous wrath.

Robert Garnier's first tragedy, *Porcie*, first published in 1568, then again in 1574 – a play that Kyd must have known, since he proposed to translate it as a sequel to his rendition of *Cornélie* in late 1593 or early 1594 (Garnier, *Cornelia*, trans. Kyd 1901, p. 102) – proclaims its civil war theme through an opening invocation of discord by the Fury Mégère. The politico-religious redeployment of the Senecan device is striking compared with its use in *Gorboduc*, even if the latter's preoccupation is likewise civil war. There it is in the Dumb Show preceding Act Four where the three Furies (Alecto, Megaera and Tisiphone) rise from hell, 'each driving before them a king and a queen' – these include Tantalus, Medea and (perhaps in compliment to Thomas Preston) Cambyses – 'which, moved by Furies, unnaturally had slain their own children' (Sackville and Norton 1976, p. 92). The origin of public discord, then, true to the Senecan model, is perverted personal passion resulting in unnatural crime. Not so with Garnier's Mégère, who lays her curse upon the whole Roman nation in envious despite of its collective 'arrogance' (*Porcie*, ed. Lebègue, 1973, l. 82):

> C'est trop, c'est trop duré, c'est trop acquis de gloire,
> C'est trop continué sa premiere victoire:
> Rome, il est ore temps que sur ton brave chef
> Il tombe foudroyeur quelque extreme mechef.
>
> [It is too much, it has lasted too long, acquired too much glory, too much continued its first victory: Rome, it is now time that some extreme adversity should fall like a thunderbolt on your haughty head.]
>
> (ll. 89–92)

The curse rolls on in 'the height of Seneca's style' for 150 Alexandrines, complete with the invocation of Alecto and Tisiphone, asked to give a respite to Tantalus, Sisyphus, Prometheus and company 'Pour faire devaler ces troupes magnanimes / De leurs mortels tombeaux aux eternels abysmes [To cause those high-minded throngs to plunge from their mortal tombs into the eternal gulphs]' (ll. 69–70).

The accomplished rhetorical performance of Garnier's Mégère is neither a laughing matter nor incongruous as the induction to a sustained tragic treatment of a Roman theme. Such high seriousness in recuperating classical mythology in service to French national preoccupations is likewise sustained in the Pléiade's most notable effort at epic, the *Franciade* of Ronsard. But the all-too-obvious French relevance of rich Roman evocations of carnage – not only by Seneca but, explicitly in the context of civil war, by Lucan – as well as the temptation to dish out religious polemic in transparent pagan guise, also exerted a strong pull on writing of a less exalted kind. This results in neo-classical deviations from high seriousness – some no doubt inadvertent, but others almost certainly not – that strike a chord with the grotesque comic element in early English tragedy.

II

In the year of *Porcie*'s first publication, Pierre Du Rosier published a verse-pamphlet entitled, *Déploration de la France sur la calamité des dernieres guerres civilles, aduenues en icelle, l'an 1568*. This is an unabashed Catholic attack on Huguenot 'rebels' as responsible for France's ills, and it is significant that the introductory sonnet[6] puts the author in the company of both Ronsard and Garnier as hurling 'vers foudrayans' at their adversaries: that is, then, what at least some contemporaries thought those two gentlemen of letters were doing at least some of the time. The mythological framework is a mingling of Christian and classical, complete with angry Jupiter, Bellona and Furies, on the one hand, appeals to 'Dieu' the 'Seigneur', on the other. Jupiter is asked why he wastes his thunderbolts on innocent rocks when he could be blasting the new race of Titans and the 'periure teste [perjured head]' of the 'Tyran' who leads them.[7] The partial answer comes in a comparison of this monster to a new Tamburlaine, 'ce grand fleau / De nostre Chrestienté [that great scourge of our Christendom]' (Du Rosier 1568, sig. B^v [p. 10]).

The villain in question is named only indirectly, but plainly enough for contemporary readers. When the rebel army is urged, 'Retirés le fer de vos propres entrailles / Et croisés sur le Turc, comme ce grand Billon [i.e. Godefroy de Bouillon] / Eternisés l'honneur de vostre Chastillon [Withdraw the sword from your own entrails and, sworn to crusade against the Turk, like that great Bouillon, eternize the honour of your Châtillon]' (sig. Ciii^r [p. 24]), the main target, already sketched in outline, comes into full view as Gaspard de Coligny, Admiral Châtillon, who was widely blamed by Catholics for igniting sectarian strife in general and the third civil war in particular, which broke out in August 1568. It is he, therefore, whom the author's wishful thinking dooms to a series of pagan underworld punishments that teeters on the brink of absurdity:

> Puis vous Demons affreus, satelites fidelles
> Du Roy Tartarean, punisseur des rebelles,
> Ne vous lassés iamais, iamais ne vous soulés
> De batre incessamment ses membres martelés
> A coups de grosse barre, & d'infecter ses leures
> De Crapaus, de Lesars, de sifflantes Couleures,
> Qui luy beuront le sang, & dedans & dehors
> Enfleront de poison son miserable corps.

[Then, you fearful Demons, faithful henchmen of the king of Tartarus, punisher of rebels, never leave off, never get enough of beating incessantly his limbs, hammered with blows of a great bar, and of infecting his lips with toads, with lizards, with hissing snakes which will drink his blood and, inside and out, swell with poison his wretched body.] (sig. Aiiii^v–B^r [pp. 8–9])

Obviously, the Christian poet, restrained, pious and humble when praying for divine mercy, takes the avowedly fictional status of the classical underworld as an imaginative licence to overkill; he can thus give retributive fantasy free rein without infringing on the principle of '*Vindicta mihi*'. The resulting mixture of both metaphysics and tones is not far from Kyd's, the speaker's impotent sorrow and rage not far from Hieronimo's.

If the neo-Senecan effect in this case is not technically dramatic, dramatic parallels are not lacking. One might take, almost at random, *La tragédie française du bon Kanut, roi de Danemark*, probably dated around 1574. This anonymous adaptation of an *histoire tragique* from Belleforest's *Cinquiesme tome* – a well-spring, as it turns out, for Danish tragedies – also targets a treacherous fomenter of civil strife in the curse of the bereaved Queen, which moves seamlessly between defining the crime in Christian terms (the murdered Canut is a saint, after all) and providing the punishment in very familiar pagan ones:

> Et toi, traître Blaccon, qui guidé de furie
> As prodigué, Judas, de ton Seigneur la vie,
> As-tu osé souiller de tes parjures mains
> Les temples jà voués aux charitables saints? . . .
> O vous, Dieux qui vengez les forfaits odieux,
> Plongez-le dans le sein des gouffres plus affreux.
> Et vengeant son forfait, pour loyer de sa peine,
> Qu'il reboulle un rocher en haut de la montaigne,
> Ou qu'au roc attaché, le<s> Thities gourmand
> Becquette ses poumons,[8] ou bien incessamment
> Rôtisse dans un feu encore telle injure
> D'un infâme tyran, d'un traître, d'un parjure.

From pathos to bathos in early English tragedy

[And you, traitor Blaccon, who, guided by fury, have let forth the life, Judas, of your lord, have you dared to defile with your perjured hands the temples once devoted to the charitable saints? . . . O you, gods who avenge heinous crimes, hurl him into the depths of the most fearful abysms. And, to avenge his crime, as the price of his punishment, let him roll a boulder back up to the mountain top, or, attached to a rock, let the ravenous Tityus peck at his lungs, or rather may it ever roast incessantly in a fire, such an offence of an atrocious tyrant, a traitor, a faith-breaker.] (ed. Lauvergnat-Gagnière, 1999, ll. 1884–1901)[9]

It is a more serious obstacle to establishing a pedigree for the dramatic hero-villain that Du Rosier's Tamburlaine *redivivus* is portrayed strictly from the outside. Still, if one were to evoke the mentality of such a ruthless overreacher, one might approach Marlowe's conception of that figure, or, for that matter, other scourges such as Barrabas or Richard III. Again in response to the outbreak of hostilities in 1568, Antoine Fleury (otherwise seemingly unknown) attacked Coligny, this time in prose, but inventing for him – the point might qualify as a milestone in literary history, were the text not so obscure – an extended self-disclosing soliloquy: 'Voila en somme le langage que le dit Admiral tient en son cueur, & dont nous voyons les desseigns & effects si confirmes, que nous n'en pouvons plus douter [Here, in brief, is the speech that the said Admiral utters in his heart, and whose designs and effects we see so confirmed that we can no longer doubt them]' (Fleury 1568, sig. Hiii^r). The combination of Machiavellism and atheism in this discourse has such a multiply familiar ring for students of early English tragedy as to justify citing it at length. The Admiral actually begins by addressing God, who, he admits, has preserved France united in the one true religion for fifteen hundred years; he then determines, however, to go his own way:

Toutesfois puis que je voy et apperçoy les hommes selon la révolution des temps tendre et incliner à changement, soit par le regard de la religion, ou de la police, et discipline civile, qui m'empeschera de troubler et pervertir l'ancienne obéissance? Et si un Mahomet de simple pâstre, s'est fait premier autheur et fondateur d'un si grand empire que celuy des Otomans: si un citadin Romain a conquis et subjugué les Gaules en dix ans: si tant de Rois ont esté despouillez par de petits compagnons de leurs subjects: Et si pour parvenir à nostre temps, un cousturier s'est faict Roi des Anabaptistes en la Germanie: si un bastard par subtils moyens s'est attribué la couronne d'Escosse: et si desia j'ay remué l'estat d'Espagne, révolté celuy de Flandres et esbranlé si avant ce Royaume, qu'un bon nombre de la Noblesse et du peuple s'est asservy et soumis à mes voluntez, pourquoy aiant un si beau subject ne pousseray-je ma fortune jusques au bout: et mesmes qu'estant vaincu je ne puis rien perdre que la teste, que j'ay ainsi par mes forfaicts engagée au roi et à la justice: vainqueur je demeure maistre de la plus grande et opulente Monarchie du monde?

[Yet since I see and perceive men tend and incline to change with the revolution of the times, whether with regard to religion, to public governance or civil discipline, who will prevent me from disturbing and perverting former obedience? And if a Mohamed, from a simple shepherd, made himself the first author and founder of such a great empire as that of the Ottomans; if a Roman city-dweller conquered and subjugated the Gauls in ten years; if so many kings have been despoiled by ordinary fellows amongst their subjects.... And if, to come to our own times, a tailor made himself king of the Anabaptists in Germany; if a bastard by subtle means has got hold of the crown of Scotland; and if I have already stirred up the state of Spain, overturned that of Flanders, and previously so shaken this realm that a good number of the nobility and the common people have subjected themselves and submitted themselves to my wishes, why, having such a splendid object, shall I not push my fortune right to the limit? And even should I be vanquished, I have nothing to lose but my head, which I have thus engaged by my crimes to my king and to justice; victorious, I remain master of the greatest and most opulent monarchy in the world. (Fleury 1568, sig. Hii^r–iii^r)[10]

This is a soberly sinister self-portrait, of course, not a grotesque caricature, and the pagan mythological machinery is missing. What would result if the Colignys of Du Rosier and Fleury were fused into one and furnished with a suitable theatrical 'world ... to bustle in' (*R3*, I.i.152)? The answer is succinctly provided by François de Chantelouve in his extraordinary dramatic apology of the Saint Bartholomew massacre, *La tragédie de feu Gaspard de Colligny* (composed 1574, published 1575), where, as far as I know (and to judge, necessarily, from the extant texts), he produced European theatre's first comic Machiavel. He did so, essentially, by dragging 'the height of Seneca's style' down to the depths, half- (but only half-) paganizing the medieval model of the hellbent blustering tyrant in a way that puts new (gnashing of) teeth into the old alliance between the energy of laughter and the awe of divine mystery.

In Coligny's opening monologue – he appears with a noose, ready to hang himself in shame at his recent defeats – the villain invokes the standard torments of the classical underworld upon himself in lines recalling the despair of Garnier's Porcie over Brutus' death (*Porcie*, ed. Lebègue, 1973, ll. 1603 ff.) – that play had received its second edition in 1574. But the underworld Coligny invokes is inhabited, not only by Sisyphus, Ixion, the Furies, and so forth, but also by Satan and Calvin, as well as his own predeceased brothers. Porcie's invitation to the pagan gods to punish 'mon chef blasphemeur [my blaspheming head]' (l. 1607) for protesting against their injustice becomes a far different matter – and approaches the 'blaspheming' of Kyd's damned Pedringano – when the punishment of Coligny's fellow heretics enters the picture: 'blasphemés en hurlemens horribles, / [aux supplices] du juste punisseur [blaspheming with horrible shrieks – / ... as He just vengeance wreaks]' (Chantelouve, ed.

From pathos to bathos in early English tragedy 43

Cameron, 1971, ll. 10–11).[11] Du Rosier's appeal to 'Jupiter' not to expend his thunderbolts on rocks is reformulated as an explicit challenge to divinity:

> ... s'il y a nul Dieu qui ait puissance adonques,
> Car en mon cœur meschant de Dieu je ne creus onques,
> Qu'il monstre son pouvoir, & darde sur mon chef
> Et non sur un rocher, des foudres le mechef.
>
> [... if there is any God upon whom to call
> (For in my foul heart I believe in none at all),
> Let him show his power, and pour upon my pate,
> Instead of some pointless rock, his thundering hate.]
> (Chantelouve, ed. Cameron, 1971, ll. 15–18)[12]

Coligny's half-ridiculous, half-horrendous daring of God out of his heaven and alliance with the powers of darkness, which he summons to swallow him up, is the standard stuff of Elizabethan theatrical villainy. It finds an especially close echo in some mighty lines of Marlowe split between the hubris of Tamburlaine and the despair of the defeated Bajazeth:

> *Tamburlaine.*
> [...]
> Stoop, villain, stoop, stoop, for so he bids
> That may command thee piecemeal to be torn
> Or scattered like the lofty cedar trees
> Struck with the voice of thund'ring Jupiter.
> *Bajazeth.* Then, as I look down to the damnèd fiends,
> Fiends, look on me, and thou dread god of hell,
> With ebon sceptre strike this hateful earth
> And make it swallow both of us at once!
> (I, IV.ii.22–29)[13]

Also to the point, though the comic potential is muted, or transmuted, is *Doctor Faustus*. Chantelouve shows the Admiral goaded into the regicidal attempt that finally provokes the king's reaction (and fulfils the divine vengeance) by a smooth-talking diabolical embassy aimed at snatching his soul. The objective is falsely to convince the Admiral of the king's responsibility for his wound, which has in fact come, more or less directly, from God (Jupiter in the thinnest of disguises). The chief ambassador is the spirit of Coligny's slain brother, Andelot, who is backed, as in *Thyestes*, by a Fury. Chantelouve's dramaturgy is avowedly Senecan here, overdetermined by way of *Thyestes* and *Agamemnon*, but it pulls all the more conspicuously in superficially contrary Christian and comic directions. And while no one could accuse Chantelouve of being less Catholic than the Pope, the play does not so much as raise the spectre of Purgatory, even if Andelot sports the '"piteous" looks' that Greenblatt would deny to 'Spirits loosed out of Hell' (2001, p. 239).

In fact, although Andelot rises from hell, he is never 'out of it', for he confesses to being tortured by alienation from 'the face of God' (Marlowe, *Faustus*, ed. Bevington and Rasmussen, 1993, I.iii.78, 79; cf. Chantelouve, ed. Cameron, 1971, ll. 901–2), and this brief respite from physical torments (Chantelouve, ll. 909–12) is overlaid on his eternal condemnation to them. In contrast to the refractory ghost of Tantalus, Andelot performs his evil willingly, thus proving himself naturally at home among the damned. He even shows himself psychologically astute, exploiting his brother's vulnerability—'Et le voyant ainsi blesphemer & desplaire, / Il sera plus enclain à ma volonté faire [And, finding him thus blaspheming, with downcast mind, / I know that to my will he'll be the more inclined]' (ll. 917–18)[14]—as well as his pride. The accompanying Fury (ll. 971 ff.), in pointed contrast to that of *Thyestes*, keeps her whips out of sight (even if she probably cannot do much about her hair), and her only speech is a parodic masterpiece of the rhetoric of persuasion, in which flattery and pleading turn on the theme of honour. Andelot and the Fury unite in absurdly obscuring the extravagant horrors to which they seek to lure their victim: Andelot actually depicts the underworld as a sort of genteel rest home where weapons are not permitted (ll. 965–68), while the Fury incongruously evokes the repose of his soul (l. 1002). The result is a thorough amalgam of classicism and Christianity, with grim humour binding them together, that precisely illustrates Hamlet's fear: namely, that the seeming spirit of that person nearest and dearest him 'may be a dev'l' that 'Abuses me to damn me' (II.ii.599, 603). Coligny's dilemma might also recall Hamlet's, in that it involves the vengeful killing of a king, although his evil nature is such that he does not hesitate for an instant.

When it comes to the pains of hell themselves, pagan fiction is again stretched to parodic limits. The Fury's reference to Andelot's reposing soul is preposterous because that character has just recited in soliloquy the ultimate catalogue of the underworld tortures to which he is everlastingly doomed. Indeed, with Andelot, Chantelouve pushes neo-Senecan infernal embellishment beyond Du Rosier's involuntary bathos, including his 'Crapaus' and 'sifflantes Couleures', into what can only be deliberate burlesque:

> Si donques je me veux reposer à mon aise,
> Je me couche en un lict couvert de chaude Braise.
> Si j'ay froid j'ay le glaz tout prest pour me chaufer,
> Et si quelque appetit a mon ventre en enfer,
> De crapaux, & Serpens, ma table plus insigne
> Se couvre, pour pouvoir appaiser ma famine.

> [If then to repose at my ease I should desire,
> I recline on a bed of coals glowing with fire.
> If I am cold, to warm me I have lots of – ice;
> And if I feel, in hell, that a meal would be nice,
> All of serpents and toads my prodigious collation
> Is made ready, which serves to keep me from starvation.]
> (ed. Cameron, 1971, ll. 881–86)

To a play that is all talk, like most French sixteenth-century tragedies, the comic extravagance of Coligny, Andelot and the several other figures of evil adds an impressive quotient of imaginative theatricality. On the one hand, that theatricality is in active service to the highest of causes, an absolute religious truth imposing a clear division between good and evil human creatures, heaven and hell. On the other hand, the recourse to pagan eschatology to validate that truth inevitably raises the destabilizing spectre of different ways of believing. The Wars of Religion, after all, were just that. Nor were they essentially foreign, either politically or ideologically, to the English spiritual experience, as scholarship is coming increasingly to appreciate. We can perhaps approach more closely by this route to historicizing the metaphysical doubt and questioning in which Elizabethan tragedy engages, not least through the comic portrayal of evil.

In its extraordinary conflation of classical and Christian mythologies and dramatic techniques, of the comic and tragic, of cosmic process and current events, Chantelouve's play is unique among the surviving texts of French sixteenth-century tragedy. The only candidate for a rough companion piece is Matthieu's *La Guisiade*. It is worth returning to the latter from several angles. For it is in that work that another component of the Elizabethan mixture, which had been part of French controversialist discourse for years, finally receives a name: the counsellors that instigate the king to his crime are explicitly termed Machiavels. Chief among them is Matthieu's equivalent of Chantelouve's Coligny, the Duke of Épernon, who, in a lengthy soliloquy, conjures the dark powers of a hell at once pagan and Christian:

> O peste de ce Tout, execrable Megere,
> Par mon ame qui t'est fidelle messagere,
> Par Cocyte et Tantal, par l'ardent Phlegeton,
> Par ces deux autres seurs Thesiphone, Alecton,
> Par le cruel Minos, par le grand Rhadamante,
> Par le poison qui sort de ta bouche beante,
> Par tant et tant d'esprits qui talonnent mes pas,
> Par le Luxe, et l'Orgueil, qui sont mes chers esbas,
> Par l'Erreur insensé, par l'infidelle Schisme,
> Par l'infecte Heresie, et le sale Atheisme. . . .

> [Megaera, of total ruin the fell harbinger,
> By my soul, which acts as your faithful messenger,
> By Cocytus, Tantalus,[15] burning Phlegeton,
> By your two sisters Alecto and Tisiphone,
> By Minos the cruel, Rhadamanthus the potent,
> By the poison that from your gaping throat you vent,
> By the numberless demons that with me consort,
> By Lechery and Pride, which provide me with sport,
> By outrageous Error, by infidel Schism,
> By stinking Heresy and filthy Atheism. . . .]
> (ed. Lobbes, 1990, ll. 867-76)

It is probably more than coincidence that Marlowe's dramatic intervention in French religious politics a few years later, *The Massacre at Paris*, violently yokes the events of Chantelouve's and Matthieu's tragedies and turns their ideological orientation inside out. Marlowe, of course, transfers the role of Machiavellian atheist from Coligny and Épernon, respectively, to the Duke of Guise – the epitome of Catholic heroism for both Chantelouve and Matthieu, and, for the latter, of martyrdom as well. The function of hero and martyr is recuperated, in accordance with long-standing Protestant hagiography, for Coligny, while Épernon becomes a loyal and respectable counsellor of his monarch. 'O Satan: o Calvin' (Chantelouve, ed. Cameron, 1971, l. 9) is virtually taken out of the mouth of Chantelouve's Coligny and given to Guise: 'Religion! *O Diabole!*' (*Massacre*, ed. Oliver, 1968, ii.63). In sum, the Prologue to *The Jew of Malta*, in announcing that Machiavelli's spirit, 'now the Guise is dead is come from France' (Pro. 3), may well be tracing, not just a moral, but also a literary pedigree.

III

The neo-classical focus of this chapter throws into relief the personage of Caesar, at once ambiguous and inescapable – an explicit presence in *La Guisiade* and *Massacre*, by turns explicit and implicit in the discourses surrounding Coligny. I therefore take this occasion to expand the issue, on the premise that it is at least as much owing to French models as to Plutarch that Caesar came to Shakespeare's hands as what the latter's Brutus makes of him – the epitome of greatness fatally tainted by ambition:

> As Caesar lov'd me, I weep for him; as he was fortunate, I rejoice at it; as he was valiant, I honor him; but, as he was ambitious, I slew him. There is tears for his love; joy for his fortune; honor for his valor; and death for his ambition.
> (*JC*, III.ii.24–29)

Such is essentially, for instance, the judgement of Montaigne: praising Caesar to the skies, on the one hand, while on the other damning 'l'ordure de sa pestilente ambition' (2.10.416[A,C]) – in Florio's translation, 'the corruption and filthinesse of his pestilent ambition' (2: 103).[16] The Protestant 'monarchomachs' are better known for pursuing the point to its logical but politically unsettling conclusion; thus the author(s) of the *Vindiciae contra tyrannos* (1579) – Théodore de Bèze? Philippe de Mornay? Hubert Languet? – assumed the identity of Junius Brutus, effectively merging the anti-Tarquinian liberator, who, in Shakespeare, inspires his descendant, with the nemesis of Caesar. But the Catholic castigators of fomenters of civil strife were there before them.

Fleury's Coligny invokes Caesar – still more damningly as the enemy of the Gauls – to serve as one of his ambitious models, and the point supports a reading of Garnier's *Cornélie*, when it was published in 1574, as an evocation of the tyrannical horror that France had just avoided, thanks to the divine retribution visited upon its would-be Caesar.[17] Although the villain's pestiferous ambition is decried in pagan terms, Garnier's heroine is allowed to introduce a remarkably Christian turn of phrase (l. 893), albeit parenthetically, in imploring the vengeance of the gods upon him – a gesture towards the mixed metaphysics pervading the more popular tradition of invective:

> J'espere que bien tost les Dieux, las de l'esclandre
> Qu'il fait journellement, broyront son corp en cendre,
> Si dans Rome trop lasche il ne se trouve aucun
> Qui vange d'un poignard le servage commun.
> Non, je verray bien tost (Dieu m'en face la grace)
> Son corps souillé de sang estendu dans la place,
> Ouvert de mille coups, et le peuple à l'entour
> Tressaillant d'allegresse en bénire le jour.

[I hope that soon the gods, weary of the outrage he daily commits, will smash his body into ashes, if Rome is so cowardly that no one may be found to avenge with a dagger the common slavery. No, I shall soon see (with God's grace) his body, fouled with blood, stretched out in the public square, cut open by a thousand blows, and the people round about bless the day, jumping for joy.] (ed. Ternaux, 2002, ll. 899–906)

It makes a revealing comment on the durability and accessibility of the political reading associating Caesar and Coligny that when Kyd translated *Cornélie* some twenty years later – virtually at the moment when Marlowe, who had just dramatically revived English memories of Saint Bartholomew, was confronted with his colleague's accusation of 'atheism' – he skewed Cicero's anticipation of Caesar's fate to make it resemble the Admiral's: 'ton corps dechiré de cent poignars aigus [your body torn by a hundred sharp daggers]' (ll. 829–30) becomes, 'And thy dismembred body (stab'd and torn) / Dragd through the streets, disdained to bee borne' (trans. Kyd, ed. Boas, 1901, III.ii.80–81).

If, with regard to Coligny, Marlowe comes to bury Caesar, he resurrects him, with a vengeance, in association with Guise. As noted in Chapter 1, that association had become widespread in contemporary commentary, proving adaptable to both negative and positive readings.[18] Marlowe comes down definitively on the negative side. His choric Machiavel moves seamlessly, in the Prologue to *The Jew of Malta*, from the Guise, to papal aspirants, to a usurping Caesar ('What right had Caesar to the empery?' [ed. Bawcutt, 1978, Pro.19]). The Henry of the *Massacre* makes the Caesarean marker a sign of vainglorious ambition and tyrannical leanings: '. . . as dictator, make or war or peace / Whilst I cry *placet* like a senator!' (ed. Oliver, 1968, xix.56–57). This matches the general French Protestant reading – witness Hurault's application, cited above (p. 10), of '*Aut Caesar aut nihil*' – but it also matches Guise's own use of the model in the soliloquy Marlowe gives him, where he resolves to dominate by means of force and fear (ii.95 ff.). It is, then, with a tyrant's blind arrogance that Guise anticipates (or perhaps echoes[19]) *Julius Caesar* in rejecting the caution offered by one of his murderers:

> Yet Caesar shall go forth.
> Let mean conceits and baser men fear death:
> Tut, they are peasants; I am Duke of Guise;
> And princes with their looks engender fear.
> (xxi.67–70)

And when the key line is recast at the moment of his death ('Thus Caesar did go forth, and thus he died' [xxi.87]), any residual grandeur is undercut by what is sordidly dragged along: a declaration of Spanish and Popish allegiance, followed by '*Vive la messe!* Perish Huguenots!' (86).

Comparable is the lesson deduced by Pierre de L'Estoile in his *Registre-journal du règne de Henri III* from the failure of 'Nembrot [Nimrod] le Lorrain' (ed. Lazard and Schrenck, 1992–2003, 3: 200) to heed the warnings and signs of his impending doom: 'tant ce grand esprit estoit avveuglé aux choses les plus claires, Dieu lui aiant bandé les yeux comme il fait ordinairement à ceux qu'il veult chastier et punir [so blinded was that great spirit to the plainest things, God having covered his eyes as He ordinarily does to those whom he wishes to chastise and punish]' (3: 198). In that Politique's eyes, the fate of the duke and cardinal was a 'Supplice digne de leur ambition, lequel, encores qu'il semble de prime face inique, voire tirannique [a punishment worthy of their ambition which, although it appears at first glance unjust, indeed tyrannical]', nevertheless manifested 'le secret jugement de Dieu [the secret judgement of God]' (3: 582). Attached to this opinion, moreover, is a reading of history that would serve perfectly well as a rationale for Brutus:

> Aussi est-il bien certain (et se void par toutes les histoires) qu'en tout grand exemple il y a quelque chose d'iniquité, qui est toutefois récompensée par une utilité publique.
>
> [Thus it is certain indeed (and is seen by all histories) that in every great example there is some element of iniquity, which is nevertheless outweighed by a public benefit.] (ed. Lazard and Schrenck, 1992–2003, 3: 202)

In *La Guisiade*, by predictable contrast, Guise's Caesarean aspect is positive, but only where the analogy is not appropriated by Guise himself. Matthieu also has to reckon with the strain of French nationalism that associated the Holy Roman emperor with the ancient invader of Gaul. Thus Guise praises the heroic exploits of his father against Charles V by condemning that 'Cesar qui foula toute la renommee / Des genereux François [Caesar, as he trampled underfoot the glory / Of the magnanimous French]' (ed. Lobbes, 1990, ll. 90–91). A useful parallel (and contrast) here is François Hotman's *La Gavle Françoise (Francogallia)*, at once anti-Roman and anti-Catholic, which comments thus on Julius Caesar's hard-won conquest: 'Ce fut certainement la destinee de ceste puissante & belliqueuse nation, qui la conduisit à ce poinct-là, à fin qu'elle fust aussi bien que les autres asuiettie à la parfin, sous la puissance de la grande Beste (ainsi qu'elle est appellee par Daniel le prophete) [It was certainly the destiny of that powerful and warlike nation which brought it to that point, so that it, as well as the others, might finally be subjected to the power of the great Beast (so is it called by Daniel the prophet)]' (Hotman 1574, pp. 23–24).[20] Matthieu obliquely self-discredits such Protestant anti-Caesarism when his d'Espernon prays for diabolical aid to destroy 'ceste vaillante race of Lorraine [that valiant race of Lorraine]', 'fort comme des Cesars [strong like Caesars]' (ed. Lobbes, 1990, ll. 883, 882).

Thus the dramatist, speaking in his own voice in the introductory 'Discours', can explicitly recuperate Caesar on Guise's behalf as a model of plain dealing and honesty against treachery:

> Aussi ce bon Prince avoit cela avec Cesar, qu'il ne vouloit point imiter la perfidie de ses ennemies, ne leur rompre la foy, ores que de leur costé ils la rompissent.
>
> [Thus that good prince had this in common with Caesar, that he would in no way imitate the perfidy of his enemies, nor break faith, although they had broken it on their side.] (ed. Lobbes, 1990, p. 69; trans. Hillman, 2005, p. 181)

And the destructive sequel of the duke's assassination will be commensurately extensive:

> Jules Cesar poignardé au Senat le laisse taint de son sang, et le genereux Duc de Guise massacré au cabinet du Roy, ne le laisse seulement empourpré des siens: mais en rend la France toute sanglante.
>
> [Julius Caesar, stabbed in the Senate, left it stained with his blood, and the noble Duke of Guise, murdered in the King's study, not only leaves the place reddened with his own but renders France all bloody with it.] (ed. Lobbes, 1990, pp. 70–71; trans. Hillman, 2005, p. 182)

The model is resoundingly endorsed in the Messenger's account of Guise's death, thanks to the final Brutus-like dagger blow personally delivered by the king: 'Ainsi mourut Cesar, ainsi mourut Alcide' (l. 2090). The Caesarean martyrdom is thereby exalted not only by an evocation of the Passion ('Reçois mon ame ô Dieu' [l. 2075]) but also by its assimilation to the Christ-prefiguring Hercules of exegetical tradition.

The concluding declamation of Madame de Nemours (cited in Chapter 2, p. 22, to evoke Henri's punishment by conscience) weaves the symbolic and rhetorical knot still more tightly. On the one hand, it makes a virtual *planctus Mariae*. On the other, it recuperates the image of Brutus, dogged by conscience, that ultimately originates in Plutarch but that Jacques Grévin's *César* (1560) had already encoded as tragic. There the destined victim vividly evokes the remorse of his prospective murderer:

> Quel honneur, quel proffit, quel plaisir, quel bienfaict
> Suyvra l'auteur premier d'un si cruel mesfaict?
> Mais plustost un remors, un remors miserable
> De la mort desireux talonnant ce coupable
> Viendra ramentevoir un antique desir,
> Allonguissant ses jours, lorsqu'il vouldra mourir,
> Se sentant trop heureux, si pour mieux luy complaire,
> On avance sa mort ainsi qu'il me veult faire.
>
> [What honour, what profit, what pleasure, what benefit shall come to the first author of such a cruel crime? Rather, remorse, wretched remorse, desirous of death, dogging the heels of the guilty one shall bring to his mind a long-past desire, prolonging his days when he wishes to die, counting himself only too happy if someone would oblige him by advancing his death, as he seeks to do to me.] (ed. Ginsberg, 1971, ll. 109–16)

It is typical of the shifting Caesarean signifier that a tragedy by Claude Billard de Courgenay on the 1610 assassination of Henri IV adapts elements used by Matthieu to exalt Guise as hero and martyr. *La mort de Henri IV* works hard to develop a parallel with the assassination of Caesar, complete with prognostications regarding the Ides of March (though the event took place in May); both Caesar and Hercules figure as models for Henri's ill-starred greatness. Still more concisely, the more distanced development of the Guisian story itself by Pierre de Bourdeille, abbé de Brantôme, the very well-connected courtier and prolific memorialist, cautions against presuming any Caesarean symbolism to be fixed or stable. His portrait of the stricken Duchess of Nemours shows her vacillating between pathetic grief and vindictiveness. Yet when, under arrest, she spies the portrait of her grandfather, Louis XII, and implores his spirit for succour, Brantôme compares her (ed. Lalanne, 1864–82, 9: 441–42), not to the avengers of Caesar, but to the original conspirators who invoked the statue of Pompey on their behalf – the very statue at whose base the Caesar of Shakespeare falls, in Brutus' view, 'No worthier than the dust' (*JC*, III.i.116). Brantôme adds, dryly:

> Possible que l'invocation de cette princesse peut servir et avancer la mort du roy, qui l'avoit ainsi outragée. Une dame de grand cœur qui couve une vindicte est fort à craindre.
>
> [It is possible that the invocation of that princess could serve and further the death of the king who had so outraged her. A lady of great spirit who nurtures a desire for vengeance is strongly to be feared.] (ed. Lalanne, 1864–82, 9: 442)[21]

Such an author is conspicuously not pursuing a sustained allegory but drawing on a common bank of fraught historical topics, which, like the rhetorical ones to which he attaches them, may be adapted to local requirements. What might appear the most firmly fixed of neo-classical signifiers thus emerges as the malleable stuff of *bricolage*. As the multiple portrayals of Henri, Duke of Guise, quintessentially reflect, the identity of Caesar, in the French political discourse that lay at varying removes behind the English, is not merely up for grabs but capable of grabbing.

IV

Arguably, then, the unrivalled potency of Caesar to signify from beyond the grave in English early modern drama owes something, however indefinite in most cases, to a pre-existing French political charge. Still, the dramatic tradition of representing Caesar in France, beginning with Marc-Antoine Muret (1547) and followed by Grévin, remains a profoundly austere one, despite the exuberant vindictiveness of Cornélie, and points in a direction tangential to the main business of this chapter. I conclude, then, by refocusing on adaptations of classical machinery to produce comic-grotesque effects.

The example of Du Rosier shows the pagan trappings of underworld punishment used as non-dramatic invective against a contemporary politico-religious enemy, and the point is well taken that even when such elements figure in plays, they do not necessarily, or simply, derive from Senecan dramaturgy. For instance, in heaping up the diverse famous torments of mythology for Andelot, on the premise that no single one would do justice to his egregious evil, Chantelouve might equally have been taking his cue from the extended poetic assault mounted by Claudian against his own contemporary *bête noire*, Rufinus, governor of the eastern Roman Empire under Theodosius and his son Arcadius. (This work was widely available in humanist editions: the two books *In Rufinum* begin the collected works of Claudian as issued by Taddeo Ugoleto in Parma, initially in 1493; they were published on their own in Vienna in 1518, edited by Philipp Gundel.)

According to Claudian, Rufinus was a monster nurtured by the fury Megaera and sent by the infernal powers to plague the world. After the bloody vengeance wrought upon his body by a mob of soldiers and citizens, his spirit descends to the underworld and comes before its judge, who is so revolted that he sentences Rufinus to undergo all the famous torments, and worse, since his crimes surpass all others (ed. Platnauer, 1976, II.498 ff.). The horrors are evoked in splendid detail, attached to the usual names, and the rhetorical excess lends the attack a satirical quality not remote from the comic grotesquery of Chantelouve or even, for that matter, of Kyd.

But this also points to the fact that the whole sequence, the spectacular meting out of vengeance in this world and the next, despite the variable and uncertain favour of the gods in the short term (II.440–41), is framed by the poet (I.1 ff.) as vindicating, not merely divine justice, but the very existence of the gods and thereby converting him from his Epicurean atheism. This is to out-Seneca Seneca himself, who, in his *Epistulae Morales* (*Letters to Lucilius*), takes Epicurus' dismissal of the infernal myths so profoundly for granted that he will not stoop to repeating it.[22] The lesson of Claudian is that the pagan lesson in its crudest forms is eminently adaptable to Christian polemic.

It is this adaptability that Ben Jonson intertextually exploited, within a framework that remains nominally pagan, when, as has been recognized by editors (though Jonson did not signal the point in his own notes), he borrowed from *In Rufinum* his vivid account of the mutilation of Sejanus by the Roman mob:

> Old men not staid with age, virgins with shame,
> Late wives with loss of husbands, mothers of children,
> Losing all grief in joy of his sad fall,
> Run quite transported with their cruelty –
> These mounting at the head, these at his face,

From pathos to bathos in early English tragedy 53

> These digging out his eyes, those with his brain,
> Sprinkling themselves, their houses, and their friends.
> Others are met, have ravished thence an arm,
> And deal small pieces of the flesh for favours;
> These with a thigh; this hath cut off his hands;
> And this his feet; these, fingers, and these, toes;
> That hath his liver; he his heart; there wants
> Nothing but room for wrath, and place for hatred.
> What cannot oft be done is now o'er done.
> The whole, and all of what was great Sejanus,
> And next to Caesar did possess the world,
> Now torn and scattered, as he needs no grave;
> Each little dust covers a little part.
> (ed. Ayres, 1990, V.824–41)[23]

The prelude to the villain's downfall is a series of divine portents, most spectacularly the averting of the face of the statue of Fortune, the only deity that Sejanus had worshipped, in true Machiavellian style. Her role is highlighted by Arruntius' sardonic rhetorical questioning in the final lines: 'Dost thou hope, Fortune, to redeem thy crimes? / To make amends for thy ill-placèd favours / With these strange punishments? (V.901–3); this translates, as editors do not seem to have noticed, an interjection in the midst of Claudian's narrative of mayhem:

> criminibusne tuis credis, Fortuna, mederi
> et male donatum certas aequare favorem
> suppliciis? una tot milia morte rependis?

[Dost thou hope, Fortune, thus to right thy wrongs? Seekest thou to atone by this meting out of punishment for favour ill bestowed? Dost thou with one death make payment for ten thousand murders?] (ed. Platnauer, 1976, II.421–23)

Nor has it been observed that Jonson was not original in adapting the passage from Claudian. In the poem, it is the soldiers that go at the corpse head-first, then the body (II.410–15), and are said to lack only scope for their vengeance (II.415–16); they then carry the pieces triumphantly on spears. Only then do the ordinary victims of Rufinus, the widows and mothers, join in, stamping on the limbs and stoning the head as it is borne aloft (II.431–35).

Jonson's rearrangement confirms what might be inferred from his making of Sejanus' fall, in part, a matter of blasphemy, namely, that he read Claudian, not just in the original (as he certainly did), but also through the adaptation that had already been made – this borrowing, too, has eluded critical notice – by the Huguenot poet Guillaume de Salluste, seigneur Du Bartas, in his rendition of the biblical Book of Judith. (*La Judit* had been translated into English by Thomas Hudson in 1584, so the deficiency in French which Jonson avowed in 1605 would not have been an obstacle.)[24] There the object of a vengeance administered by the true God on behalf of his chosen people is the pagan tyrant Holofernes, who undergoes mutilations unprecedented in the biblical account, first of the severed head, then of the body. When Judith first brings the head back to Bethulia, it is set up on the wall – Jonson's mention of the people 'mounting' at the head of Sejanus, which has provoked editorial puzzlement,[25] may well reflect this – whereupon

> . . . les peres, les fils, les pucelles, les vefves,
> Tristes d'avoir perdu par les ethniques glaives
> Leurs enfans, leurs parens, leurs amis, leurs espoux,
> Esperdus de tristesse et fumantz de courroux,
> Pellent son menton palle, esgratignent sa face,
> Crachent dessus son front, arrachent de sa place
> La langue qui souloit mesme outrager les cieux
> Et d'un doigt courroucé luy pochent les deux yeux.

[. . . the fathers, sons, maidens, widows, grieving at the loss to the pagan swords of their children, their parents, their friends, their husbands, wild with sorrow and fuming with anger, dig at his pale chin, scratch his face, spit on his forehead, rip from its place the tongue that was accustomed to defy heaven itself and with a furious finger gouge both his eyes.] (ed. Baïche, 1971, VI.215–22)[26]

The mutilation of the body takes place later, after the Hebrew victory over the discomfited Assyrian host, when the headless corpse of Holofernes is discovered on the battlefield and torn, not merely limb from limb but, as in Jonson, though not Claudian, atom from atom, by a vulgar mob lacking only scope for vengeance and eager for souvenirs:

> Car il n'a nerf, tendon, artere, veine, chair
> Qui ne soit detranché par le sot populace
> Et si son ire encore ne trouve assés d'espace. . . .
> Il n'y a dans Jacob si malotru coquin
> Qui de sa chair ne vueille avoir quelque lopin.

[For there is no nerve, tendon, artery, vein, or piece of flesh that is not sliced off by the foolish populace, and even so their anger does not find enough scope. . . . In all the tribe of Jacob there is no rascal so crude but he will have some little bit.] (ed. Baïche, 1971, VI.310–12, 317–18)

In all three texts, the sequence concludes with the ironic contrast between the tyrant's vast ambition and the little room, less than a grave, now needed for his remains (Claudian, II.47 ff.; Du Bartas, VI.345 ff.), although Du Bartas, naturally, points the moral in Judaeo-Christian terms: 'O grand Dieu . . .' (VI.345). Still, the classical roots of Du Bartas's epyllion of vengeance show through, as when the doomed Holofernes falls drunkenly asleep and intuits the punishments awaiting him in the next world:

> Ja se tourne son lict, ja mille clairs brandons
> Luisent devant ses yeux, ja dix mille bourdons
> Bruyent dans son oreille. Il voit des Minotaures,
> Meduses, Alectons, Chimeres et Centaures.

[Now his bed whirls round, now a thousand bright torches glow before his eyes, now ten thousand hummings buzz in his ear. He sees Minotaurs, Medusas, Alectos, Chimeras, and Centaurs.] (ed. Baïche, 1971, VI.97–100)

Likewise, Rufinus 'diu curis animum stimulantibus aegre / labitur in somnus [whose mind had long been a prey to anxiety, sank into a troubled slumber]' (Claudian, II.326–27) and had intimations of his death presented by the ghosts of his victims. And when Holofernes is dead, we are told that he, 'deja, miserable, / A passé du noir Styx la rive irrepassable [already, wretched, has passed over the bank of the dark Styx, which can never be crossed again]' (Du Bartas, VI.251–52).

Undoubtedly, we are in the realm of commonplaces, but they are acting, and interacting, so as to generate some fairly specific meanings, which, moreover, cross and re-cross the Channel. For if Jonson, the most rigorously and self-consciously neo-classical of English Renaissance playwrights, rewrote Claudian's exuberant verbal vendetta in light of Du Bartas's earnest *exemplum* of divine justice visited upon an atheistic criminal, a blasphemer, and an enemy of the truth, he had a French theatrical precedent even for such rewriting. We return once more to Chantelouve. *La Judit* swells the crowded ranks of controversial texts published just prior to *Colligny*, to which it stands in polemical opposition. Given Du Bartas's religious affiliation, it would have been clearly understood, according to the contemporary encoding of political-religious issues, that the chosen people delivered by divine intervention represented the Huguenots.

The specific symbolism of Holofernes' miraculous demise before the walls of Bethulia was already in place: the allusion was to the 1563 assassination of François, Duke of Guise, which rescued the besieged Protestants in Orléans – a murder widely attributed to Coligny's instigation.[27] So it is by Chantelouve (ed. Cameron, 1971, ll. 52–54, 235–37), as one of the egregious crimes for which Saint Bartholomew was divine retribution, and he tailors the rhetoric of one of his Protestant villains accordingly: 'Judith n'a elle pas d'une main annoblie, / Detesté le Tyran pour sauver Bethulie? [Did not Judith, with a hand divinely uplifted, / To save Bethulia cut off the tyrant's head?]' (ll. 499–500). It is, then, across the narrative intertext of *La Judit* that the militant Catholic playwright recuperates the vindictive lesson of Claudian for his blaspheming Huguenot tyrant, who, by the grace of God, is finally beheaded, mutilated and made to point, upside-down, the same ironic moral about his need for space:

> Il estimoit l'onde
> Les terres, le monde,
> Petites pour luy,
> Et or sa chair vaine
> Par la boüe traine,
> Sans los aujourd'huy.
>
> [He thought the huge sea,
> Every territory,
> For him was too small;
> Now his vain flesh and blood
> Is made in the mud –
> And in scorn – to sprawl.]
>   (ed. Cameron, 1971, ll. 1179–84)[28]

Yet Chantelouve's Coligny is also something that Du Bartas's villain is not: a fortune-worshipping Machiavel aspiring to royal power. To this extent he intertextually displaces Holofernes as a link between Claudian's Rufinus and Jonson's Sejanus, and also attracts, like Sejanus, the ironic moral along what might be termed its vertical axis:

> Bref, & celuy qui desiroit la France
> Seigneurier, en son desir felon,
> Est possesseur, ô divine vangeance,
> Du plus haut lieu qui soit en Mont-faulcon.
>
> [And so, on that traitor whose spirit showed
> To lord it over France such appetite,
> Vengeance divine has finally bestowed
> Possession of Montfaucon's greatest height.]
>   (ed. Cameron, 1971, ll. 1185–88)[29]
>
> For whom the morning saw so great and high
> Thus low and little, 'fore the'even, doth lie.
>   (*Sejanus*, ed. Ayres, 1990, V.912–13)

In this form, the moral has ample classical precedents, including Senecan ones.[30] But a highly specific link, if it is not palpable, can almost be smelt.

From pathos to bathos in early English tragedy 57

Jonson's tragedy hinges on the turning away of Fortune during Sejanus' ceremony of propitiation. The audience would have witnessed the rites described in the elaborate stage direction (V.183S.D.); these culminate in the offering of incense, the 'begging smoke' (V.82) that Sejanus has declared himself, however grudgingly, willing to offer to her alone among the gods. The violent reaction of Sejanus picks up this element and tinges his atheism with the comic grotesque:

> Nay, hold thy look
> Averted, till I woo thee turn again;
> And thou shalt stand to all posterity
> Th'eternal game and laughter, with thy neck
> Writhed to thy tail, like a ridiculous cat.
> Avoid these fumes, these superstitious lights,
> And all these coz'ning ceremonies. . . .
> (ed. Ayres, 1990, V.194–200)[31]

In his final soliloquy, Sejanus dares, like Chantelouve's Admiral, 'you, that fools call gods' to 'let me be struck / With forkèd fire' (V.390, 397–98).

The Admiral, too, has problems with Fortune:

> O souveraine Royne, & princesse du monde,
> Qui le piéd mal-certain tiens sur la Boule Ronde,
> Que t'ay je fait affin d'ainsi me renverser . . . ?

> [O most sovereign queen and princess of the
>   world,
> Who keep uncertain footing as the globe is whirled,
> What have I done to you to be thus overthrown . . . ?]
> (Chantelouve, ed. Cameron, 1971, ll. 63–65)

In determining, as Fleury had put it previously for him, to '[pousser] ma fortune jusques au bout', Chantelouve's Coligny effectively anticipates Sejanus' desperate resolution – 'Mais courage, ceux là qui n'ont plus d'esperance, / Fichent tout leur espoir sur la desesperance [But courage: those who have no further hope yet dare / To stake a kind of hope even upon despair]' (ll. 99–100) – and promises the goddess the same offering if she will turn his way again:

> Que si à mes desirs tu respond, o fortune!
> Mon invincible cœur fera la mort commune,
> Et n'estant point ingrat d'Encens je couvriray
> Tes autels, & l'odeur aux astres envoiray. . . .

> [If only, O Fortune, you deign to grant my prayer,
> My invincible heart will spread death everywhere,
> And, since I'm not stingy with incense in the least,
> From your altars I'll send the stars a fragrant feast.]
> (Chantelouve, ed. Cameron, 1971, ll. 103–6)

There used to be a perfume advertisement that went, 'Promise her anything, but give her....' The respective sequels offer dramatic, highly theatrical proof that Lady Fortune in both Chantelouve and Jonson is quite capable of recognizing such promises as *de la fumée*, which is another way of saying that there is nothing truly heavenly about her.

The point is not that Jonson may also have known the tragedy of Coligny. (This is hardly impossible, although the kind and degree of his knowledge would obviously depend on the extent of his knowledge of French in 1603.) Again, we are dealing with commonplaces – and the most common of places, by proverbial definition, is Rome, to which all roads lead, or at least led. In the case of early modern English tragedy, however, the conclusion seems inescapable that one of those roads – which also, of course, led away from Rome – passed through Paris.

Notes

1 Editors also find a comic echo of Clarence's ghost in Shakespeare's *R3*, V.iii.124–25.
2 See below, n. 22.
3 What for me is the crucial question of jarring metaphysical systems is commonly sidestepped in discussions of Senecan elements in early modern English tragedy, including the broadly comparative survey of Braden (1985), whose approach is predominantly rhetorical, philosophical and (in the general sense) psychological. Thus, too, Miola takes Aaron for granted as at once 'swaggeringly Senecan' and descended from 'other progenitors including the Machiavel and Vice' (1992, p. 27). He does not deal with the possible inflection of Senecan influence on English practice by 'parallel uses on the Continent' (p. 10). Seneca does not figure at all in the most recent full-length study of the diabolical tradition in English drama, that of Cox (2000).
4 On the place of Giraldi Cinthio's *Orbecche* in the Senecan tradition generally, see Braden 1985, pp. 115–23.
5 Hence the title of Thomas Lodge's play (*c.*1587–92) dealing with the wars between Marius and Sulla, a precedent the French did not fail to apply to their own situation (although not, as far as is known, in dramatic form).
6 Signed 'Iaqves Moysson'. Page numbers are those of the BnF digitalized facsimile of Du Rosier's poem.
7   Et toy grand Iuppiter, qui portes en tes mains
       Les traits Vulcaniens pour punir les humains,

> Pourquoy vois tu silent ceste pariure teste,
> Que tu ne la gremis [sic – 'gémis'?] d'vne iuste tempeste?
> Et auec ce Tyran, sa race, à celle fin
> D'eteindre tout d'vn coup vn genre si mutin,
> Dresse toy contre luy, ride ton front seuere,
> Enfonce tes sourcis, enflambe ta colere,
> O grand Saturnien, & n'amuse tes bras
> A batre les Rochers qui ne t'offencent pas . . .

[And you, great Jupiter, who bear in your hands the Vulcanian darts to punish human beings, why do you silently regard that perjured head and not growl upon it with a deserved storm? And with that Tyrant, his breed, so as to extinguish at one stroke such a mutinous race, rise up against him, wrinkle your dreadful forehead, contract your brows, inflame your anger, O great Saturnian, and do not sport your arms with battering the rocks that do not offend you . . .] (DuRosier 1568, sig. Aiiii^{r-v} [pp. 7–8])

8 As Lauvergnat-Gagnière suggests (1999, n. to 1898), the legend of Tityus, whose liver was devoured in the underworld, has evidently been misunderstood.

9 This play has been preserved only in two manuscripts; there are some indications of performance, perhaps under Jesuit auspices. The political target has been identified as Henri III's rebellious brother, François, Duke of Alençon (later of Anjou), leader in 1574–76 of the mixed religious 'Malcontents'. See Lauvergnat-Gagnière, Introd., 1999, pp. 3–8; cf. Jouanna, Boucher, Biloghi et al. (eds) 1998, pp. 231–36. However, when the *histoire tragique* first appeared (1570), Belleforest probably had Coligny in mind, if not also Henri de Navarre – see *French Reflections*, Chapter 3.

10 The fictive monologue is also cited by Crouzet 1994, p. 473, as an example of the discourse deployed against Coligny in the years prior to the Saint Bartholomew massacre.

11 The line numbers of my published translation, cited throughout, correspond to those of Cameron's edition (1971).

12 Du Rosier is also more straightforwardly echoed by Chantelouve's Chorus in ll. 301–6 (ed. Cameron, 1971).

13 *Tamburlaine the Great* (Parts I and II) is cited throughout in the Revels edition of Cunningham.

14 Cf. *Faustus*:

> For when we hear one rack the name of God,
> Abjure the Scriptures and his Saviour Christ,
> We fly in hope to get his glorious soul,
> Nor will we come unless he use such means
> Whereby he is in danger to be damned.
>   (ed. Bevington and Rasmussen, 1993, I.iii.48–52)

15 The notorious punishments of Tantalus ('Tantal') in the underworld would make him a virtual embodiment of the horrors of hell. Still, the other names in the line

are geographical, and this seems a possible printer's error for 'Tartarus' ('Tartare').
16 Cf. Montaigne, ed. Villey, 1965, 2.33.729–33(A); trans. Florio, 1965, 2: 457–62.
17 I develop this point in my translation of *Colligny* (2005). See the Introduction, pp. 36–41, as well as the corresponding passages signalled in the notes.
18 Cf. Weil 1997, pp. 87–88, 98, and 198n.29, on some resonances of the 'Caesarism' of Marlowe's Guise; for a reading in terms of 'epic masculinity' exposed, cf. Shepherd 1986, pp. 157–60.
19 Oliver (ed.) conjectures that a post-1599 reporter 'switched on to the wrong track' (1968, p. lvii) and altered a Marlovian evocation of the well-known association between the Guise and Caesar. It is also possible that both plays echo an earlier text now lost or that Shakespeare here took his cue from Marlowe.
20 See Dan. 7:3–17. Cf., however, the 1568 Protestant characterization of Charles IX as a discord-fostering Pompey, opposed to the Caesarian Prince of Condé, providentially destined to bring peace to the state (Crouzet 1994, pp. 478–79).
21 I have not encountered further references specifically implicating the Duchess of Nemours in the king's assassination; on the other hand, the Duchess of Montpensier, Guise's sister, was widely credited with orchestrating the event, although this idea has been questioned (Bourassin 1991, p. 203): she was said to have regretted afterwards only that Henri was unaware of her involvement (Chaintron 1988, p. 53).
22 See letter 24.18, ed. Reynolds, 1965:

> Non sum tam ineptus ut Epicuream cantilenam hoc loco persequar et dicam vanos esse inferorum metus, nec Ixionem rota volvi nec saxum umeris Sisyphi trudi in adversum nec ullius viscera et renasci posse cotidie et carpi: nemo tam puer est ut Cerberum timeat et tenebras et larvalem habitum nudis ossibus cohaerentium. Mors nos aut consumit aut exuit.
>
> [I am not so foolish as to imitate the Epicurean prattle on that subject, and I affirm that fears of the things below are idle; neither is Ixion turned on a wheel, nor is a rock thrust forward by the shoulders of Sisyphus, nor could anyone's entrails be plucked out and renewed every day. No one is such a child as to fear Cerberus and the places of darkness and the ghostly state of those holding together with mere bones. Death either consumes us or strips us bare.]

23 See Ayres (ed.) 1990, nn. to V.824–42 and 828; cf. Herford, Simpson and Simpson (eds) 1925–52, n. to V.814–32 (vol. 9).
24 See his Epigram in praise of Josuah Sylvester's 1605 translation of *Bartas his Deuine weekes & workes* (*Epigrammes*, 132 [Herford, Simpson and Simpson (eds) 1925–52, 9:83]). As often, it is hard to know whether to take Jonson at his word, but it would seem that he at least improved his French subsequently. While Drummond of Hawthornden states that Jonson did not know French or Italian (*Conversations*, ed. Donaldson, 1985, 4.55–56 [p. 596]), he also records him as

From pathos to bathos in early English tragedy 61

criticizing Sylvester's Du Bartas, which he had commended before he knew better (3.21–22 [p. 595]). Donaldson terms Drummond's dismissal 'almost certainly an exaggeration' (n. to 4.55–56 [p. 759]).

25 See Ayres (ed.) 1990, n. to V.828.
26 Baïche's edition, cited throughout, is based on the author's revised version of 1579, which was multiply reprinted. Incidentally, if Jonson did not consult the French, his 'digging' nevertheless corresponds strangely to 'Pellent'; there is no equivalent in Claudian, or in Hudson's translation of Du Bartas:

> There, fathers came, and sonns, & wives, & mayds,
> who erst had lost amongst the *Heathen* blayds,
> There sonnes, their parens, maks, & louers deare,
> with heauie harts & furious raging cheare.
> They pilde & paird his beard of paled hew,
> Spit in his face & out the toung they drew,
> which vsde to speak of God great blasphemies,
> And with their fingers poched out his eyes.
> (ed. Craigie, 1941, VI.213–20)

27 On the typological reading of the event, see Jouanna, Boucher, Biloghi *et al.* (eds) 1998, p. 120. Agrippa d'Aubigné, too, invokes it in *Les tragiques*, ed. Lestringant, 1995, 5.381–86. On the political symbolism of Du Bartas's poem in particular, see Baïche (ed.) 1971, pp. xxi–xlvii. In the *Histoire ecclésiastique des églises réformées du Royaume de France* (attrib. to Théodore de Bèze), the actual assassin, Poltrot de Méré, has a notably Judith-like moment in which he prays that God may either change his purpose, if the act is not according to the divine will, or give him the constancy and strength to kill the 'tyran' and deliver Orléans from destruction (1974, 2: 349).
28 In turn, the Huguenot pamphlet *Le tocsin contre les massacreurs* (1577) seems virtually to be re-imagining Coligny's fate through that of Rufinus when it describes the treatment of the body at the hands of the Parisians: 'ils portèrent le tout [tête et parties honteuses] sur des bastons par la ville et l'exposait ignomineusement en vente à qui en voulait [they bore all (head and private parts) on sticks through the city and exposed it for sale to whoever wanted any]' (cited Postel 2004, p. 186).
29 Montfaucon, outside Paris, was the site of the public gallows, where Coligny's mutilated body was displayed in grotesque mockery. The irony was recorded approvingly by many Catholic partisans.
30 See Ayres (ed.) 1990, n. to V.912–13.
31 The alignment here of the atheist Sejanus with a quasi-Protestant disdain for superstition suggests a Catholic tinge to Jonson's treatment.

4

Staging the Judith jinx: heads or tales?

Since around the end of the twentieth century, war has again broken out as a favoured topic in the criticism of early modern English drama, and it is perhaps not coincidental that a culture of war has simultaneously returned to prominence, if not dominance, not least in English-speaking societies. The still-entrenched New Historicist and Cultural Materialist presumption of mimetic complicity between an age's political occupations and its intellectual preoccupations seems determined to validate itself. In any case, that presumption, by and large, has governed recent approaches to early modern theatrical warfare: an impressive array of contemporary cultural documents on military subjects has been mustered, then pressed into the service of textual explication. The orientation is broadly but overwhelmingly materialist, on the premise that the early modern conceptualization of war is generated by warfare as a cultural practice.

One can only be grateful for the fruitful juxtapositions often effected by such criticism. Still, conclusions as to the instability, ambivalence, or outright subversiveness of the theatrical imagining of war, especially by Marlowe and Shakespeare, recur with a regularity that imparts a feeling of the foregone – and tends to foreclose the cultural distance that justifies the exercise in the first place. Moreover, despite occasional gestures towards matters continental or farther afield, the roll-call of intertexts tends to be narrowly Anglocentric. This seems an artificial limitation for a period when, against the background of the French civil wars (and other European conflicts that were more or less related), historical narratives and *mémoires* with substantial military content, several authored by eminent soldiers, were proliferating across the Channel. (One has only to think of Blaise de Monluc,[1] Philippe de Mornay, Brantôme, and Symphorien Champier – all of whom I cite either in this volume or in *French Reflections* – but there are others: François de la Noue, Martin Du Bellay, Gaspard de Saulx-Tavannes, Vieilleville [François de Scepeaux].) Finally, the insistent materializing of ideology has tended to marginalize the metaphysical archetypes and images through which the most material of issues habitually obtruded, in Elizabethan society, upon the production and reception of knowledge and culture.

My main purpose here is to propose that perhaps the most culturally prominent instance of a combined metaphysical and military narrative, the biblical encounter between the Jewish heroine Judith and the Assyrian tyrant Holofernes, hovers intertextually in the background in two 'warrior plays' by Shakespeare and Marlowe, respectively. The basic story was hardly obscure. It was available in all the major versions of the Bible, even if designated as apocryphal in Protestant ones (the Council of Trent had reaffirmed its canonicity for Catholics). The English plays, however, appear particularly to depend on Du Bartas's dynamic, richly embroidered, and both theologically and politically charged retelling, especially when it comes to one highly functional addition: the warrior's suspect self-presentation in and through inflationary narrative.

Du Bartas, of course, applies the biblical account so as to affirm God's convenant with man in the cause of Reformed Christianity. The poet's militant Protestantism was the key to his extraordinary popularity in England, and *La Judit* begins by acknowledging its origins in a commission by Jeanne d'Albret, Queen of Navarre, herself a plausible type of Judith. As previously mentioned, from the first publication of the poem in 1574 (two years after Jeanne's death), it was read as endorsing the miraculous deliverance of God's chosen people from a host of ungodly foreigners (Spanish and German troops formed part of Guise's army at Orléans). The model was naturally adaptable, and duly adapted, to other Protestant underdogs resisting Catholic 'tyrants': Catherine de Parthenay's play of *Holoferne* (most regrettably lost) was staged during the Catholic royalist siege of La Rochelle in 1572; *Le miroir des vefves, tragedie sacrée d'Holoferne et Judith* (by the schoolmaster Pieter Heyns) was performed at Antwerp ten years later.[2] In this way of thinking, it was a small and natural step from Jeanne d'Albret to Queen Elizabeth (precisely, in fact, the trajectory traced by Marlowe in *Massacre*), and from the Duke of Guise to Philip II of Spain. Thus it is hardly surprising that the anonymous writer of a 1578 pamphlet reporting on the struggle of the Dutch against Don John of Austria concludes with a prayer applying the Judith/Holofernes paradigm along these lines.[3]

La Judit of Du Bartas had been very frequently republished, and in 1582 it began appearing with an uncompromising Calvinist commentary by Simon Goulart, thereby acquiring fresh currency and stature as a militant Protestant tract. Hudson's translation included arguments and summaries reflecting the thrust of Goulart's glosses. I have elsewhere proposed that the circumstances of its production (it is one of the few documented results of the sojourns in

Edinburgh during the early 1580s of the London-based – and government-connected – Huguenot publisher Thomas Vautrollier) point to English intervention in the propaganda battle for the heart and mind (and indeed the body) of the young King James VI of Scotland.[4] (The latter was then also being subjected to Guisian blandishments, literary and otherwise, but proved highly susceptible to intellectual flattery and was already inclined to admiration of Du Bartas.) Little is known about Thomas Hudson, except that he was one of four brothers of English origin in the king's service as musicians, but it is highly suggestive that his brother James 'acted as the go-between for James VI. in his dealings with the English government from the date of the king's escape from the Ruthven Raiders in 1583 till the Union of the Crowns in 1603' (Craigie (ed.) 1941, pp. xi–xii, n. 3). Using resonantly Reformist language in dedicating his translation to James as '*him who God in goodnesse hath erect / For princely Piller, to his owne elect*' (I.15–16), Hudson presents the work as a royal command performance, even as a partial collaboration, though also as a purely literary endeavour – confirmation of the porous boundary between artistic and political activity in the early modern context (when perhaps Beauty was actually Truth and Truth Beauty).

I

Du Bartas's retelling fleshes out the biblical account in every sense, and it includes a vivid evocation of the seductive arts mutually practised by both Judith (calculatingly) and Holofernes (naively) during their encounter. On the other hand, the human dimension is tightly woven into a theological fabric – from the multiple sinful condition of Holofernes, which marks him as cast off from grace, to the miraculous moment of truth victorious. In the Book of Judith (13:8), the heroine, after praying for strength but in the full knowledge that she is fulfilling the divine will, nevertheless requires two strokes to cut off the head of Holofernes. In Du Bartas's account, she first falls into moral doubt, then resolves to cut her sleeping enemy's throat (a more practical procedure than decapitation, after all), only to lose heart and tremble with 'womanly' fear. Through prayer, however, she gets instant and spectacular results: 'puis si roidement frape sur le vis-roy / Qu'heureuse elle depart avec l'ethnique lame / Le chef d'avec le corps et le corps d'avec l'ame [then she struck at the king's lieutenant so soundly that she produced the happy result of parting, with the pagan blade, the head from the body and the body from the soul]' (ed. Baïche, 1971, VI.154–56). The poet is not about to contradict the Bible outright, but he gives the distinct impression of a single blow manifesting a sudden and irresistible miraculous force.

In keeping with Du Bartas's double perspective – frail humanity and divine inspiration – part of my objective here is to reincorporate the mimetics of ideology, including gender relations, within a religious perspective. The discourses of war and politics in the period confirm such a mixture as quintessentially early modern, yet the (post)modern view tends to reduce religion to one discursive phenomenon among at least near equals – witness even such an adroit analyst as Nick De Somogyi: 'biblical and classical sources strengthened the association of war with rumour' (1998, p. 133). In fact, the discourse of European warfare in this period almost invariably turns on a religious axis – recognizably, at bottom, the rhetoric of crusade, but fragmented, democratized, open to appropriation – on the paradoxical premise that the exercise of power over life and death is human practice but divine prerogative.

The disparate elements in that mixture may, of course, be provisionally separated. So they are, for instance, in *A watch-worde for warre*, a treatise occasioned in 1596 by a renewal of the Spanish-Catholic menace, in which Charles Gibbon systematically treats the various branches of his subject first from one point of view, then from the other. But the two perspectives finally conjoin under the sign of transcendent truth: for him the figure of Judith is taken to manifest human anomaly, namely the 'courage of a woman', but as a manifestation of divine strength (1596, sig. C2^v). It is a myth that matches, of course, the paradox of a female ruler supernally endowed with masculine (hence, potentially emasculating) strength. Such doubleness, I suggest, is deployed ironically and backhandedly in *Othello* and *Tamburlaine*, where, in the conspicuous absence of divine mission or guidance, two vulnerably human Judiths *in potentia* succumb to the destructive charms of their respective incarnations of Holofernes.

The anomaly of Judith as an icon of godly virtue has the potential to cut especially deeply, given that the very womanliness by which she exercises her courage is regularly cast in spiritual terms as dangerous and debasing. Early modern English theatre had a predilection for emblematic encounters between warriors and women, most of which, of course, ring straightforward changes on the Samson motif: masculine duty meets effeminizing desire, with a bad or good outcome depending, respectively, on male vulnerability or resistance. In Judith's case, exceptionally, a contrary response is called for, which palpably goes against the moral and cultural grain: the more desire she provokes, the better for her divine mission. Her symbolism is thus imbued with a destabilizing potency – hence my coinage of the 'Judith jinx', the experience by avatars of Holofernes of a seductive femininity transcendently equipped to turn their swords against them.

The point may be illustrated by the very early association of Judith with Jeanne d'Arc by French writers and illustrators. Olivier Bouzy traces to this root an emblem of chastity who is also 'plus ou moins amoureuse et érotisée [more or less inclined to love and eroticized]' (2000, p. 242).[5] That paradox proved so unstable that it lent itself to those who sought to discredit Jeanne – as the English and their allies were quick to do with their label of 'putain'. In following suit, however, Shakespeare (or whoever developed the character of Joan de Pucelle in *Henry VI, Part One*) re-enfolded her sexuality into her magical power. It may be the strongest testimony to the potency of the Judith model that, in contrast with its invocation by Holinshed (where it is conjured, though only to be discarded [ed. Bullough, 1957–75, 3: 172]), Shakespeare keeps the name of Judith out of the mouths of even Joan's warmest admirers.

II

Of the two English tragedies in question here, it is convenient to begin with *Othello* on account of the concise, highly charged ambiguity with which it exploits the model. This it does, arguably, by playing it off against its biblical mirror image: the encounter between Samson and Delilah. Among the ambiguities of the relation between Othello and Desdemona to which an audience is rapidly sensitized is the doubtful truthfulness of the hero – thanks, paradoxically enough, to the mediations of a blatant liar who passes for 'honest'. Yet so much recent criticism (including some of my own)[6] has bolstered the idea of Othello's construction of his own identity through narrative, with the more or less tacit support of the postmodern shibboleth that 'truth' is never stable or absolute, that the blurring of the question in the play has been largely reproduced in commentary. Naturally, we have come to think, Othello invents himself through language, since that is what we all do. The point is fair enough in itself, but it happens to go squarely against the insistence of all the characters that the truth can be determined, and that it matters. (Iago makes the *telling* exception here: 'what you know, you know' [V.ii.303] serves as a fitting epitaph for one who, with regard to his own wife, actually prefers suspecting to knowing.)

The fact is that Shakespeare added the story-telling element, with its problematization of truth, to Cinthio's plain tale: in *Gli Hecatommithi*, the Moor's heroic past is objectively recorded, while the Lady's attraction to him has nothing to do with his narrative powers (ed. Bullough, 1957–75, 7: 244). The effect of the addition is to sway the primary biblical model of Samson, seduced with difficulty into telling the truth about his strength,[7] in the direction of Holofernes – specifically, the Holofernes invented by Du Bartas, who believes that his seductive potency depends on his boasting.

The business of getting at the truth begins with the Venetian Senate's judgement of Brabantio's accusation and Othello's defence about the wooing of Desdemona, and so does the evidence that the truth has not been got at. First, objectively speaking, the *ad hoc* quasi-judicial hearing is perfunctory and biased, since the pressing 'affairs of state' (I.iii.220) to which Othello is essential clearly take precedence over the father's private grievance. Then, Othello himself moves quickly away from objective speech, as his refutation of one 'witchcraft' (169) enters into the service of another. Over a mere fifteen lines or so – the play's famous 'double time scheme' arguably begins at this level – his autobiography progresses from down-to-earth soldierly adventures ('hair-breadth scapes i' th' imminent deadly breach' [136]) to mythical landscapes ('hills whose heads touch heaven' [142]) to the most notorious extravagances of travellers ('men whose heads / Do grow beneath their shoulders' [144–45]). 'I think this tale would win my daughter too' (170), the Duke responds, and it is hard not to suspect Ben Jonson of a pioneering critical comment when, two years later, in a play devoted to debunking the travellers' fabrications of Sir Politic Wood-be, he showed a Venetian judge prepared to be gulled by Mosca: 'A proper man! [*Aside*] And, were Volpone dead, / A fit match for my daughter' (*Volpone*, ed. Parker, 1983, V.xii.50–51).

But then Othello's first words in his defence (I.iii.83) make the dubious claim that his active military career began at the age of seven – roughly the age when even Volumnia's grandson, that chip off the Coriolanian block, is still mammocking butterflies ('One on's father's moods' [*Cor.*, I.iii.66]). And an audience is arguably predisposed, in proportion as it wavers in credulity regarding Othello, to lend some credence to Iago – notably, when he adapts Othello's wooing narrative to the desires of his dupe Roderigo: 'Mark me with what violence she first lov'd the Moor, but for bragging and telling her fantastical lies. To love him still for prating – let not thy discreet heart think it' (II.i.222–25). It compounds the irony that the initial image of magical wooing is at least seriously qualified in the direction of Venetian courtship, when Desdemona pleads for

> Michael Cassio
> That came a-wooing with you, and so many a time,
> When I have spoke of you dispraisingly,
> Hath ta'en your part. . . .
>
> (III.iii.70–73)

By the time Othello relocates 'magic in the web' (III.iv.69) of his lost handkerchief, again swiftly escalating his narrative – fewer than twenty lines take him from the plausible hearsay of the Egyptian 'charmer' (57) to a 200-year-old sibyl (70–71) and 'mummy . . . / Conserv'd of maidens' hearts' (74–75) – the most gullible audience is at least as likely to echo Desdemona's questioning ('Is't possible?' [68]; 'is't true?' [75]) as to credit Othello's affirmations ("Tis true' [69]; 'Most veritable' [76]). All of this leads up to the climactic submerging of story-telling within actuality in the account of the 'circumcised dog' that Othello 'smote' 'in Aleppo once' because he 'Beat a Venetian and traduc'd the state' (V.ii.352–56). The veracity of this final tale enacts itself in the present, before eye-witnesses, in a way that conspicuously relegates to irrelevance any claim to past truth.

Boasting and lying are traditionally, of course, comic signs of military false pretences, as in Shakespeare's more obvious variations on 'the figure of the Braggart', by which, as De Somogyi observes, he 'seems to have been absorbed' (1998, p. 179):[8] Parolles, who indeed proves nothing but words; the 'swaggering' Captain Pistol, who gets his shameful comeuppance at the hands of Fluellen; Falstaff himself, whose very resourcefulness in inverting cowardice and heroism ('is not the truth the truth?' [*1H4*, II.iv.229–30]) ultimately serves the interests of the state, despite his best efforts. Such inversions work to affirm the stability of the categories and the proportionality of their signifiers: truth is to lies as bravery is to cowardice. It says much about the chief beneficiary of Falstaff's discursive practice that Henry V is at first (as Hal) willing to 'gild' Falstaff's 'lie' about having killed Hotspur (*1H4*, V.iv.157–58), and that he continues to see value in disjunctions between appearance and reality: the anonymous veteran of Agincourt will be no less heroic for remembering 'with advantages / What feats he did that day' (*H5*, IV.3.50–51); Fluellen's silly flamboyance, which might well be hollow braggardism, harbours 'care and valor' (IV.i.84).

As a general Shakespearean rule, however, true heroics go hand-in-hand with true speaking, and if disproportion is threatened, special witnessing is called for. The heroism of Coriolanus would seem incredible, except as Cominius will 'report it' (*Cor.*, I.ix.2), and even the grudging Citizens will be compelled by his scars 'to put our tongues into those wounds and speak for them' (II.iii.6–7). The extraordinary blood-shedding of Macbeth requires testimony from a 'bloody man' (*Mac.*, I.ii.1): 'He can report, / As seemeth by his plight, of the revolt / The newest state' (1–3); 'So well thy words become thee as thy wounds, / They smack of honor both' (43–44). And paradoxically, Antony's heroic depths are brought vividly to the surface when he excoriates himself for cowardice in seconding Cleopatra's flight (*Ant.*, III.xi).

In fact, Othello is unique among Shakespeare's warriors in never being called upon, until his last desperate moment, to display the valour for which he is virtually metonymic (the 'warlike Moor Othello' [II.i.27], 'our noble and

Staging the Judith jinx: heads or tales?

valiant general' [II.iii.1–2]). The issue is ironically counterpointed by his own repeated insistence on 'ocular proof' (III.iii.360) in testing the truth of his 'fair warrior' (II.i.182). That the question is current, and the stakes high, is backhandedly confirmed by the frivolous banter (regularly cut in performance) at the opening of Act III, Scene iv between Desdemona and the Clown, who refuses to tell her where 'Lieutenant Cassio lies' (III.iv.1–2) – Othello's deadly serious plays on the word 'lies' are anticipated (IV.i.34 ff.) – on the grounds that 'He's a soldier, and for me to say a soldier lies, 'tis stabbing' (5–6).

III

When Othello casts himself at once as the chastiser of the 'circumcised dog' and as that dog himself, he enacts precisely his ambiguous status as defender of Venetian Christianity and outsider within it. Less often discussed is his choice of circumcision as a sign of difference. Neither the word nor the idea occurs elsewhere in Shakespeare, but the cultural and religious resonances are particularly rich in the dramatic context. These begin with the suggestion that Othello himself may be circumcised (as a presumed convert to Christianity from Islam – and as Desdemona may or may not know). But also to the point is his invocation of the Old Testament distinction between God's chosen people and their enemies; in these terms, too, he is poised between two identities: the hero of Christianity (according to which the sign of circumcision has been replaced by baptism) and an 'erring barbarian' (I.iii.355–56), as Iago puts it, applying the same pun on 'erring', as will be noted, that Du Bartas uses for Holofernes.

Othello from the first has figured himself as a sort of Samson, Dedesmona as a Delilah *in potentia* (headgear making a particularly sensitive point for cuckolds-in-waiting):

> ... when light-wing'd toys
> Of feather'd Cupid seel with wanton dullness
> My speculative and offic'd instruments,
> That my disports corrupt and taint my business,
> Let housewives make a skillet of my helm....
> (I.iii.268–72)

And it is indeed a version of Samson's fate that he incurs, in his own estimation, when, victimized by a deceitful woman, he loses his manhood, bidding farewell in a single breath to the 'tranquil mind' and to his 'occupation': the 'Pride, pomp, and circumstance of glorious war' (III.iii.348–57).

The emasculation of the Hebrew warrior by the Philistine woman who wheedles out the secret of his strength was, of course, the common stuff of Renaissance legend, fusing neatly with the myths of Omphale subduing

Hercules, Venus disarming Mars. Thus, when Antony, Hercules' direct descendant, cries that Cleopatra 'has robb'd me of my sword' (*Ant.*, IV.iv.23) – thereby echoing Othello's 'I am not valiant neither, / But every puny whipster gets my sword. / But why should honor outlive honesty?' (*Oth.*, V.ii.243–45) – he enacts a virtual synthesis of the *exempla* amassed by Spenser in *The Faerie Queene*:

> Nought under heaven so strongly doth allure
> The sence of man, and all his minde possesse,
> As beauties lovely baite, that doth procure
> Great warriours oft their rigour to represse,
> And mighty hands forget their manlinesse;
> Drawne with the powre of an heart-robbing eye,
> And wrapt in fetters of a golden tresse,
> That can with melting pleasaunce mollifye
> Their hardned hearts, enur'd to bloud and cruelty.
>
> So whylome learnd that mighty Jewish swaine,
> Each of whose lockes did match a man in might,
> To lay his spoiles before his lemans traine:
> So also did that great Oetean knight
> For his loves sake his lions skin undight:
> And so did warlike Antony neglect
> The worlds whole rule for Cleopatras sight.
> Such wondrous powre hath wemens faire aspect,
> To captive men, and make them all the world reject.
> (ed. Dodge, 1908, V.viii.1–2)

As for Shakespeare's œuvre, such potential has lain in the warrior identity as early as *Love's Labour's Lost*, whose Don Armado, a *miles gloriosus* once (if not twice) removed, consoles himself for his obsession with Jacquenetta by invoking the precedents of both Hercules and Samson (I.ii.57 ff.).

At the same time, even the model of Samson, as applied to Othello, has a trenchant double edge. That strongman's undoing by Delilah represented the ultimate retribution of the Philistines for the great destruction he had wrought upon them, which began with his seemingly unnatural – but in truth divinely inspired – choice of a wife from among their dominant culture:

> Then his father and his mother said vnto him, Is there neuer a wife amonge the daughters of thy brethren, and among all my people, that thou muste go to take a wife of the vncircumcised Philistims? And Samson said vnto his father, Giue me her, for she pleaseth me wel. But his father and his mother knewe not that it came of the Lord, that he shuld seke an occasion agaynste the Philistims: for at that time the Philistims reygned ouer Israel.
> (Judg. 14:3–4)

Indeed, Samson first yielded to a woman's blandishments when he told his wife the answer to a riddle. The upshot was his killing of thirty Philistines, whereupon 'Samsons wife was (giuen) to his companion, whome he had vsed as his friend' (14:20). This, in turn, so offended Samson that he destroyed the Philistines' fields with fire and thereby provoked their killing of his wife and her father, which then afforded him another occasion for revenge. The divinely appointed champion of the circumcised may have been doing the Lord's work all along, but his heroic stature is no simple matter: it is implicated in sexual desire and jealousy across cultural boundaries, inversely related to truthful self-revelation, and ultimately self-destructive.

Of course, Othello finally proclaims himself the ferocious destroyer, not the champion, of the circumcised, and in Old Testament terms, this is to stamp him as a virtual anti-Samson. The archetypical biblical encounter with the emasculating woman thereby takes on another fictional overlay, as if by anamorphosis, and Othello looms, however dimly, as Holofernes. It is perhaps not gratuitously, given its own running theme of the battle of the sexes – of men who yield to women but also of women who both resist and dominate men – that *Love's Labour's Lost* actually gestures nominally towards that biblical intertext, which subtends the discourse of boastful and unrighteous militarism throughout the period. That play's Holofernes is hardly a warrior – his name most immediately derives from that of Gargantua's tutor, with whom he has some ridiculous traits in common.[9] But even as he contrasts with Don Armado, playing the absurd epitome of the *vita contemplativa* as opposed to the *vita activa*, he joins with him in the Pageant of the Nine Worthies.[10] There indeed he casts himself in the role of Judas Maccabaeus, like Samson, the circumcised antithesis of his biblical namesake. There, too, all the make-believe Worthies are finally cut down to size. But so are those who initially laugh at them – the Lords converted by dint of sexual desire from their delusions of superhumanity into vows of spiritual reformation in the shadow of death. For the ladies have, in a sense, made trophies of all their heads, turning back their attempted seduction by mirroring to them their very seat of pride as a mere *memento mori*. We witness collectively, in effect, the power of the Judith jinx.

Shakespeare's plays never actually mention the biblical Judith, although he gave that name to his second daughter.[11] (This was apparently in friendly homage to Stratford friends, but the fact that he had named his first daughter Susanna establishes the apocryphal heroines as a familial motif.) It may be argued, however, that Othello's self-casting at once as biblical hero and villain in his own pitiful pageant of the Worthies could hardly have failed to evoke the image of the archetypal 'fair warrior' for audiences of the period. The phrase seems tailor-made for Judith, and with pathetic irony to reverse her triumph. 'The tragic loading of this bed' where Desdemona had been awaiting her bridegroom anew is the 'work' (V.ii.363–64) of the play's 'demi-devil' (301), and it parodically displaces the divinely comic biblical denouement.

In the Book of Judith, the Assyrian horde is thrown into consternation by the inverse discovery. They find their general's decapitated body in his bed, where he had with equal wishful thinking been awaiting Judith, until he fell drunkenly asleep. Thanks to Iago, Othello, priding himself on self-control and fearful of Samson's destiny, has revealed himself as Holofernes despite himself, an 'erring barbarian' ferociously triumphing over a 'circumcised dog'. This is in sharp intertextual contrast with the joyful circumcision, at the conclusion of the biblical book, of the Ammonite Achior, who had been expelled by Holofernes to Bethulia for prophesying the Assyrians' defeat and who recognizes the severed head of Holofernes as the sign of the God of Israel.[12]

IV

The story of Judith constituted a particularly rich and contested symbolic field in late sixteenth-century religious and political discourse. This fact has perhaps been obscured by the Reformers' formal relegation of the biblical book to the Apocrypha, despite the fact that Luther himself deemed it to be a godly and edifying history (actually having its origins, as he thought, in drama).[13] But for the English, the most widespread and influential retelling was undoubtedly that of Du Bartas, which, apart from its multiple French editions, received a further English translation after that of Hudson (by Josuah Sylvester in 1614, belatedly for my present purposes).[14]

It is uniquely in the version of Du Bartas that the figure of Holofernes, whom the Book of Judith makes a straightforward embodiment of military ferocity and enmity to Israel, acquires his affinity with the *miles gloriosus* and, at length, a propensity for narrative self-fashioning. The bulk of Du Bartas's embellishment is devoted to Holofernes' extravagant accounts of his far-flung exploits and adventures, with which Judith encourages him to suppose he may seduce her. These super-abundantly fill a mere gap in the biblical account (Judith 12:16–20), where Holofernes has virtually nothing to say – just too much to drink. In rich and exotic colours, the Holofernes of Du Bartas is made to paint a larger-than-life portrait of himself as, in effect, an 'erring barbarian', with the poet ironically imposing a frame of Iago-like scepticism:

> Holoferne reprend ses derniers erremens,
> Et fait un long recit de ses deportemens,
> Moitié vray, moitié faux. Les bravaches gen-d'armes
> Mentent le plus souvent parlant de leurs faicts d'armes.

Staging the Judith jinx: heads or tales? 73

[Holofernes took up his latest wanderings and made a long story out of his doings – half true, half false. Boastful warriors are most often liars when they speak of their deeds of arms.] (ed. Baïche, 1971, V.439–42)

In the case of Du Bartas's character, truth-telling and religious truth quite specifically go hand-in-hand, or tongue-in-tongue. Holofernes' propensity for narrative self-aggrandizement is bound up with his blaspheming, for which he is posthumously punished.

One of Du Bartas's further significant supplements to the biblical account is the amazing series of mutilations of Holofernes' body, which include tearing out his tongue for 'mesme outrager les cieux [speak(ing) of God great blasphemies]' (ed. Baïche, 1971, VI.221; trans. Hudson, ed. Craigie, 1941, VI.219). It is to the point, perhaps, that Othello most immediately chastises the 'circumcised dog' he has become for the verbal offence of having 'traduced' the Christian 'state'. In both cases, too, the blind denial of truth generates intimations of the dismal destiny of the guilty soul. Desdemona, lying about her murderer out of love, before she is revealed as Judith rather than Delilah – hence, indeed the 'fair warrior' he had once believed her to be – is initially Othello's candidate for damnation: 'She's like a liar gone to burning hell' (V.ii.128). When Emilia proves her true identity, hence his own false one – 'O, the more angel she, and you the blacker devil' (130) – it is his own infernal torments that he summons up:

> Whip me, ye devils,
> From the possession of this heavenly sight!
> Blow me about in winds! roast me in sulphur!
> Wash me in steep-down gulfs of liquid fire!
> (V.ii.277–80)

This is an especially complex moment intertextually. Certainly, Othello's Senecan *furor* here, as effectively brought out by Miola (1992, pp. 124–43, esp. p. 138), confirms the Herculean self-image, too, as a pivot: the hero raging against his feminization has suddenly been revealed to himself, as in an anamorphic self-portrait, as the unwitting wife-killer. But his language also sustains the Judaeo-Christian framework, and on this ground he meets with the doomed Holofernes, awaiting Judith's divine stroke with dim and confused glimpses of the torments in store for him (see Chapter 3, p. 55).

Othello, unlike Holofernes, is hardly in a drunken stupor, but, ironically, he has fallen into a similar barbaric rudeness while shunning the very vices that go along with it, according to Du Bartas's insistent moralizing: lust and drunkenness. Both of these he ostentatiously disclaims and denounces – and is encouraged by Iago to project upon Cassio, as he is encouraged nevertheless to feel himself indelibly barbaric by comparison. Othello ultimately becomes his own anathema by mistaking Desdemona, in her simplicity, for a 'cunning whore' (IV.ii.89), as the 'tyran' does Judith, when she artfully appears to him in the seductive guise of Cleopatra:

> A son oreille pend une perle plus riche
> Que celle qu'avala la princesse peu chiche
> De Memphe aux hautes tours.
>
> [From her ear hung a pearl richer than that swallowed by the lavish princess of high-towered Memphis.] (ed. Baïche, 1971, IV.53–55)

Hudson highlights the spiritual symbolism in making the pearl 'of greater vallewe' (ed. Craigie, 1941, IV.55); his gloss likewise insists on the moral dichotomy—and anticipates Othello's language: '*Cleopatra*, the concubine of *M. Antonius*, who swallowed a rich pearle'.

Indeed, in so far as Othello's failure to recognize a true pearl when he sees one invalidates his Samson-like self-image, one might suppose him more likely to be thinking of himself as a 'base Judean' (Q1) than a 'base Indian' (F1) who 'threw a pearl away / Richer than all his tribe', to invoke the famous textual crux of V.ii.347–48.[15] 'Judée' recurs in Du Bartas' poem (as in other Old Testament narratives) for the Jewish homeland and people; 'Iuda' is still more frequent in Hudson, who also translates 'villes et provinces' (I.354) as 'tribes and townes'. Insistently, in thoroughly Calvinist fashion, the contrast is between 'l'ost incirconcis [folke vncircumsisde]' (I.318 [trans. Hudson]) and the Jews who are willing to die for their faith, 'comme fit Samson [As Sampson did]' (I.267 [trans. Hudson]), because they truly know their value as the *elect* of the divine will. Othello falls prey to Iago – who to Roderigo identifies himself with 'all the tribe of hell' (I.iii.357) but for Othello's benefit ironically prays, 'Good God, the souls of all my tribe defend from jealousy!' (III.iii.175–76) – because the Moor's faith depends on his fragile sense of belonging to the right tribe, the (symbolically) circumcised. Such faith would mean profoundly accepting that Desdemona 'saw Othello's visage in his mind' (I.iii.252), that 'she had eyes, and chose me' (III.iii.189). It is not the only Shakespearean instance where faith makes the antidote to jealousy ('It is requir'd / You do awake your faith' [*WT*, V.iii.94–95]), and if the flirtation in *The Winter's Tale* with 'superstition' (43) in the form of the moving statue has sometimes conjured Shakespeare the Catholic for faith-hunting critics, what Huguenot intertextuality tends to reinforce as *Othello*'s psychological adaptation of Reform theology may serve as a lesson in ecumenism.

At the moment in *La Judit* when the elect status of the Jews is most resoundingly reaffirmed, as Achior tells Holofernes their true story at the opening of Book II, Samson is cited again as proof of God's power to preserve them, even though 'l'Autan, depopulant ses landes, / Fit venir en ton camp toutes ses noires bandes' (II.375–76). And at this point, the language of Hudson's translation becomes especially difficult to exclude from the intertextual field: '... though south *Autan*, would dispeople his lands, and bring the blackest *Mores* to swarm in bands'. As is far from irrelevant to the anamorphic Othello, the crucial distinction between a Samson and a Holofernes suddenly emerges as quite explicitly a matter of white and black.

V

The paradigmatic story of Judith seems also to have inflected another early modern encounter between a chaste woman and a brutal stranger, and this encounter may also have resonated, in its turn, behind the Shakespearean scene. (It also resonates with, if it did not actually suggest, the name of the redoubtably resolute virgin of *Measure for Measure*, who comes close to saving her maidenhead, after all, at the price of the head of her unchaste brother.)[16] The *Orlando Furioso*, too, has been neglected by criticism as an intertext for *Othello*, but it is not unlikely to have been recalled by audiences at the moment of the heroine's murder.

The ruse by which Isabella in Canto Twenty-Nine thwarts the lust of Rodomonte ('barbaro crudel [cruel barbarian]' [ed. Caretti, 1966, Stanza 11]) and triumphs as a virtuous widow has long been recognized as lying at some distance behind that of Olympia in Part Two of *Tamburlaine* (IV.ii): there Marlowe's captive tricks Theridamus into stabbing her in the neck by pretending, like Isabella, to demonstrate an ointment conferring invulnerability. It is not quite, however, 'the same stratagem',[17] since in Ariosto the sleight involves decapitation. The latter motif is the key to an active evocation, through inversion, of the biblical pattern: the drunken stupor of the poem's Saracen (who is of elevated status – the King of Algiers – but, of course, ungovernable passions) aids Isabella's purpose and makes him an 'erring barbarian' by his own confession: Rodomonte is left alive but profoundly deploring 'suo errore [his error]' (Stanza 30) – a thorough victim, it might be said, of the 'Judith jinx'.[18]

In the (notably free) 1591 translation of Ariosto by John Harington, the intertextual presence of Holofernes actually takes on a colouration matching that provided by Du Bartas, who sternly insists that one degradation leads to another, lust to gluttony and drunkenness ('Venin plus que la peste aux guerriers dangereux, / Tu vas effoeminant les cœurs plus genereux [Poison more dangerous to warriors than the plague, you render effeminate the most noble hearts]' [ed. Baïche, 1971, VI.17–18]). Ariosto himself does not belabour Rodomonte's other fleshly vices, but Harington, whose rhetoric at this point reduces the character to a 'grosse Pagan' (trans. Harington, 1591, Bk. 29, Stanza 24) and 'beastlie Turk' (29.26, 32), seemingly as devoid of royal status as of the fear of God (29.10), pointedly scorns Rodomonte's 'drunken surfet' (29.32) and supplies the Canto with a moralizing appendix to the same effect: 'In Rodomonte we may see the effects of inconstancie, sensualitie and drunkenes.'[19] Harington's Isabella, incidentally, emerges as especially Desdemona-like: 'both wife and continent and chast, / Of faultlesse manners, and of spotsesse fame' (29.31).[20]

What is perhaps more surprising is that a more recent French dramatic treatment of Isabella's death at the hands of Rodomonte succinctly fills a gap in the usually cited Shakespearean sources. I have more to say in *French Reflections*, with regard to *Antony and Cleopatra*, about the plays of Nicolas de Montreux, including *La tragédie d'Isabelle*, whose first publication dates, apparently, from 1595. Its particular interest for *Othello* lies in Montreux's parallel development of the murderer's remorse in the direction of suicide. On the one hand, the Moor in Cinthio's source story, when he realizes his mistake, wishes to kill only the villainous Ensign, not himself. On the other hand, in the *histoire tragique* of Bandello that is plausibly cited as the origin of several details of the climax, the jealous wife-murderer madly kills himself as well, but 'abhorred to the laste mynute of his lyfe the remembrance of repentance'.[21] Montreux, who constructs his tragedy wholly around Isabelle's death, not only develops the violent remorse of his Rodomonte ('Il maudit sa folie, il blasme son erreur [He curses his madness; he blames his error]') well beyond the original in Ariosto,[22] but has those in attendance disarm him to prevent his suicide:

>   . . . vn chacun le fer des poings lui tire,
>   Sans armes on le laisse acoiser seul son ire,
>   Il demeure esploré, la chaste dame il plaint,
>   Il prise sa vertu, estime son los sainct,
>   Morte il veut l'honorer, qu'il auoit voulu viue
>   Forcer, diffamer, rendre au deshonneur captiue.
>
> [. . . together they tear the sword from his hands; unarmed they leave him to calm his anger alone. He remains in tears; the chaste lady he pities; he prizes her virtue, values her sacred worth. Dead he seeks to honour her, whom living he sought to force, to defame, to render captive to dishonour.] (Montreux 1595, p. 81 [Acte V])

This Rodomonte might as well complain, 'I am not valiant neither, / But every puny whipster gets my sword' (*Oth.*, V.ii.243–44). In this version, too – uniquely, it would seem – his destructive jealousy is provoked by hearing Isabelle speak of another man, and in the spirit that Othello merely imagines in Desdemona's talk of Cassio:

Staging the Judith jinx: heads or tales? 77

> Tousiours estoit le nom de Zeobin en sa bouche,
> Nom triste & desplaisant au Barbare farouche,
> Barbare qui fasché d'vne si longue erreur,
> Commençoit a changer son amour en fureur.

[Always the name of Zeobin was at her lips, a name troubling and displeasing to the fierce barbarian, the barbarian who, angered at such prolonged misconduct, began to transform his love into frenzy.] (Montreux 1595, p. 86 [Acte 5])

Finally, if the 'Turk' of Harington's translation is effectively displaced by Shakespeare onto the *alter ego* invented by Othello in his speech of self-destruction, that fact, too, at least happens to correspond to Montreux's procedures. For while, in adapting the episode from Ariosto, the French playwright to some extent recuperated Rodomonte's royal dignity – an element matching the paradoxical nobility of Shakespeare's 'barbarian' – he also echoed the reductive epithet employed by Cinthio for his protagonist: 'More cruel [cruel Moor]' (Montreux 1595, p. 90 [Acte 5]).

VI

I turn now to *Tamburlaine*, whose intertexts are notoriously complex, and where the question of multiple sources, as raised in the Introduction, comes into play. As for the Judith paradigm, however, at a basic level it recapitulates and reinforces the sharp contrast between divine prorogative and 'atheistic' challenge that has always defined Marlowe's protagonist. The point here is that the (over-)loading with Truth of the Judith/Holofernes paradigm simultaneously invests it with enormous subversive potential. That is why it can equally be invoked to powerful effect by the ungodly forces of regicidal evil, as in Chantelouve's *Colligny*.[23] Such potential, I would suggest, is also unleashed when Marlowe – who in *Massacre*, more than incidentally, makes Du Bartas ('Bartus') a spokesman for divine vengeance as Navarre's follower – '[dares] God out of heaven with that atheist Tamburlan'.[24] The story thus makes an equally fraught, if low-key, counterpart to the resonances of Revelation that have caught critical ears (Weil 1997, p. 201n.35; Gibbons 1990, pp. 218, 222).

Naturally, much has been said about Tamburlaine specifically as a warrior – the approach was pioneered by Kocher (1942) – as well as about the surprisingly versatile deployments of the personage prior to Marlowe. He came to Marlowe already well adapted to illustrate, with teasing ambiguity, both Machiavellian efficacity (*virtù*) and divine scourging. The latter function, moreover, was itself well established as a wild card. For if English allusions to Tamburlaine tend, not surprisingly, to 'shore up agendas that, however contradictory, point towards greater nationalism' (Shepard 2002, p. 21) and the militant Protestantism associated with it, other nationalisms had staked prior claims on the Catholic side.

As has been seen, for Du Rosier in 1568, Admiral Coligny appeared as a new Tamburlaine, 'ce grand fleau / De nostre Chrestienté' (sig. B^v, p. 10), who ought to be crusading against the Turks rather than stirring up strife among Christians. The anti-Turkish card was rather more indirectly played, but likewise from an anti-Protestant hand, some thirteen years later by Fronton Du Duc, who juxtaposed the English depredations in France during the Hundred Years War with an oriental parallel, in order to make the standard point about divine scourging:

> Or ceci se faisait lorsque vers le levant
> Ce roi turc Bajazet les chrétiens poursuivant
> Battait Constantinople et que ce grand tartare
> Vainqueur le châtia de son désir avare,
> Ce fléau du genre humain, Tamerlan, qui si tôt
> De rustaud se fit roi pour l'effort de son ost
> Traînant un million de soldats qui saisie
> Lui mit en son pouvoir presque toute l'Asie.
>
> [Now, this all happened at a time when, in the east,
> That King of the Turks, Bajazeth, who never ceased
> Harrying Christians, battered Constantinople; then
> It was the turn of that great Tartar to chasten
> Him in battle for his greed: Tamburlaine, that scourge
> Of humankind, who, from a peasant, cresting the surge
> Of a million soldiers, made himself king in a day,
> Enforcing nearly all Asia under his sway.]
> (ed. Prévost, Pro.47–54; trans. Hillman, 2005)

For Fronton Du Duc, this is background to the emergence of Jeanne d'Arc as the Catholic saviour of France – on the model, explicitly and insistently, of Judith (ll. 47–54, 712–13, 1598–1601, 2390 ff.).

VII

Such background becomes Marlowe's foreground, its basis the material compiled from various sources by the Spaniard Pedro Mexía and included in the latter's series of meditations on (divinely inflected) natural and human history. This is the work known in the French translation of Claude Gruget as *Les diverses leçons de Pierre Messie* – a relevant point because, by nearly universal agreement, it was by way of Gruget that Marlowe arrived at Mexía.[25]

Scholars have differed, however, over the route he took, not to mention the various byways that may have led him to supplementary details.[26] The earlier tendency was to privilege the English translation of Gruget (openly acknowledged as such) by Thomas Fortescue in *The Foreste* (published in 1571, then again in 1576); latterly, the pendulum has swung towards the passages from Gruget adapted (without acknowledgement) by George Whetstone as a (very small) part of a rambling assault against Envy and Popery, entitled, *The English Myrror*. This work's more recent appearance (1586) seems more likely to have inspired Marlowe's choice of dramatic subject. Cunningham, in the Revels edition, judges this to have been 'convincingly demonstrated' (1981, p. 10).

The situation does not appear to me so clear-cut, given that, unlike Fortescue, Whetstone freely condensed his restricted adaptations of Gruget and did not include one substantial chapter formally dedicated to the phenomenon of the scourge of God, with Tamburlaine duly enrolled as an example.[27] On the other hand, while Fortescue generally rendered chapters of his original fully, he also left out a great many, as he acknowledges in his 'Epistle Dedicatorie' (1571, sig. aiij^v), including one focusing on the Turkish empire, in which Bajazeth's forced abandonment of the siege of Constantinople and humiliating service as Tamburlaine's footstool are recounted.[28] Given these respective omissions, it seems strange that critics have taken so little account of *Les diverses leçons* itself.[29] The latter was, after all, a very well-known book, circulating, by Marlowe's day, in multiple editions produced by several French publishers. Moreover, beginning, it would seem, in 1577, the translations of Mexía by Gruget (who had died around 1560) began to appear with extensive supplements by Antoine Du Verdier, seigneur de Vauprivaz. These include, in a chapter on suicides, an account of Bajezeth's degradation and self-destruction (Mexía 1580, 2: 158–59) that comprises a fairly close digest of the passage from Petrus Perondinus (*Magni Tamerlanis Scythiarum Imperatoris Vita* [1553]) long accepted as Marlowe's source for the same details.[30] All this would be beside the point here, except that Marlowe in some places appears to supplement Whetstone from Gruget, and there is no particular reason to assume his recourse to Fortescue.

VIII

Marlowe's radical application of the floating signifier of Tamburlaine as scourge involves, I suggest, attaching it intertextually to the absolute inflexibility, in spiritual terms, of the encounter between the blaspheming Assyrian tyrant and the Jewish heroine. To the extent that Tamburlaine is made specifically to evoke Holofernes, the absence of any candidate for the role of chosen people, hence ultimately for the transcendent *chooser* of that people, is thrown into relief. So is the absence of a heroine divinely inspired to risky enterprise in defence of her country. Cunningham terms Marlowe's invention of Zenocrate 'perhaps the most striking extension of his source-material' (1981, p. 20) – that is, of the historical and biographical accounts of Timur; it is all the more so for introducing into that fable of irresistible masculine force a Judith *manquée*, truly seduced rather than deceitfully seducing – losing her own head, as it were, while Tamburlaine keeps his (the more impressively because it verbally teeters for a moment on his shoulders).

When Shakespeare, ten years or so after Tamburlaine's English stage debut, parodically appropriated the military and geographical prodigies of Marlowe's conqueror in representing Pistol as a *miles gloriosus*,[31] he was harking back to origins. The extravagant oriental landscape depicted with the brushstrokes of Marlowe's mighty line and punctuated with evocatively exotic place names would have been a novelty for audiences as a backdrop to Tamburlaine's conquests, but, however embellished from Ortelius and other recent sources,[32] it was well established in association with those of Holofernes, another notably well-travelled tyrant. Indeed, allowing for the relative historical and geographical precision of Marlowe – for the treatment of time and place in the Book of Judith is notably indefinite (not even Bethulia can be confidently identified with a real place) – the two cartographic spaces overlap considerably. The vast territory swarms with some of the same peoples (Persians, Moors, Arabs, Parthians and, of course, Hebrews), and it is staked out, with similar sonority, by a number of the same landmarks: Judaea, Arabia, Babylon, Syria, Damascus, Persia, Media, Egypt, Ethiopia, the Euphrates, the Danube, the Euxine sea – and with particular resonance, however obliquely, Scythia (a point I will return to). Sonority itself becomes a vector of intertextuality.

The intertextual presence of the Judith story, laden with symbolic significance, ensures that the metaphysical question – in essence, that of true and false gods – remains active when *Tamburlaine*'s universe is at its most reductively physical. This notably includes a detail that has been held to show Marlowe's privileging of 'the technology of victory' over 'theology' (De Somogyi 1998, p. 70). Undoubtedly, Marlowe shows expertise in military techniques, especially those of siege warfare; among these, as signalled by Kocher (1942, p. 218), is the cutting off of food and water – witness both Bajazeth at Constantinople (I, III.1.58 ff.) and Techelles at Balsera (II, III.iii.29 ff.). Thirst, in particular, is a classic and natural weapon of war in a desert climate, as the Bible illustrates elsewhere, although De Somogyi (1998, pp. 68–70) also considers that the use of the stratagem at Rabath by the forces of David under Joab, as dramatized by Peele in *David and Bethsabe*, enacts the reimposition of theology upon technology.[33] In any case, what remains a side issue in the story of David is at the very core of that of Holofernes and Judith. Both in the biblical original and in Du Bartas's narrative, the seizure of Bethulia's water supply by Holofernes is at once an effective tactic and a supernatural scourging, hence a prelude to the revelation of divine favour.[34] For it is the resulting suffering – powerfully, if sparely, evoked in the original, and infused with ghastly detail by Du Bartas (ed. Baïche, 1971, III.283–320) – that elicits Judith's bold initiative.

IX

As with *Othello*, it is crucially telling that, in Du Bartas, Holofernes himself does the telling. The epyllion restructures the direct and concise biblical narrative to begin *in medias res* with Holofernes' descent upon Israel. The background to this invasion, the war between the Assyrians and the Medes, is thoroughly transformed by being incorporated into the boastful recital that Judith urges Holofernes to deliver, encouraging him to suppose that she is drinking in every word, as Othello at least supposes Desdemona to have been doing. (This is, of course, in order to defer the Assyrian's amorous intentions and get him to drink too much.) The transformation involves at once diminishing and distancing the role of his royal commander-in-chief, Nabuchodonosor. According to this Holofernes, it was his own intervention that won the battle against the Medes (in the biblical narrative, he has not yet even been mentioned at this point). He provides an account worthy of the eyewitness in *Macbeth* ('Doubtful it stood . . .' [*Mac.*, I.ii.7 ff.]), presenting the combat as uncertain until he himself arrived on the scene 'comme un foudre [like a thunderbolt]' (ed. Baïche, 1971, V.374) to rescue the cause of his king: as Macbeth 'carv'd out his passage' (19), so for Holofernes his enemies' pieces of armour, 'devant mon coutelas[35] / Sont fresles comme verre [before my short-sword are frail as glass]' (V.376–77). Indeed, Macbeth's treatment of the chief rebel – he 'unseam'd him from the nave to the chops' (22) – is anticipated in reverse: 'Cetuy-ci d'un fendant / Je vais depuis le chef jusqu'au ventre fendant [Him with a cleaving blow I split from the head to the belly]' (V.383–84).

Macbeth's prodigious feats of ferocity do not figure in Holinshed's account, and one might conjecture that the ultimate beheading of that 'tyrant' (the word is used fifteen times for Macbeth, hardly ever in the other late tragedies) led Shakespeare to depict him, too, so as to evoke the tyrannical Holofernes. In any case, the rhetorical similarity points to the precedent in Du Bartas for the 'joie sauvage, une forme de jouissance perverse [savage joy, a form of perverse sexual thrill]' identified by François Laroque (1990, p. 31) in various Shakespearean and Marlovian descriptions of butchery in battle. The precedent stands out, moreover, for turning that perversity back on itself.

Holofernes' campaign against the Jews enacts Nabuchodonosor's vengeance against those who had failed to support the king in his previous war. The Book of Judith cites Nabuchodonosor at length as he grandiosely gives Holofernes his bloody marching orders – and makes clear who is boss: 'And take thou hede that thou transgresse not any of the commandements of thy Lord but accomplish them fully, as I haue commanded thee, and differre not to do them' (2:13). Holofernes is *de facto* delegated as the scourge of God, 'for it was enioyned him to destroy all the gods of the land, that all nacions shulde worshippe Nabuchodonosor onely, and that all tongues and tribes shulde call vpon him as God' (3:8). In Du Bartas, by contrast, Nabuchodonosor is all but cut out of the picture; in the midst of his narrative, Holofernes devotes a few bare lines (ed. Baïche, 1971, V.426–30) to receiving his orders, then launches into a self-glorifying account of his own exploits, beginning with his inspirational address to his army. In reporting this discourse (without biblical warrant), and the enthusiasm with which it infused his soldiers, he proves a plausible model for Tamburlaine. Central to the parallel is the impression that the scourge, not least in his own view, eclipses the god.

Certainly, as in various battles of Tamburlaine, the attack on Israel will test the power of the enemies' God, whom Holofernes has dismissed as an invention of Moses ('Un dieu qu'à son plaisir ton Moïse a forgé [A god your Moses has fashioned as he pleased]' [ed. Baïche, 1971, II.416]), thereby anticipating Marlowe's opinion according to Richard Baines. But Nabuchodonosor's name is not mentioned; the soldiers are roused to warlike fury by and for Holofernes; indeed, the glory of an earthly crown is part of the spoils he promises them, in rhetoric that appropriates apocalypse:

> 'Vengés le plus grand dieu qui descendit jamais
> Des cercles estoilés. Armés, soldats, armés
> L'une main d'une torche et l'autre d'une lame
> Pour gaster l'Occident et par glaive et par flamme.
> Couvrés d'une mer rouge et ses monts et ses vaux.
> Faites dedans le sang nager vos fiers chevaux.
> Recevés bienheureux le sceptre et la couronne
> De ce grand univers, qui tout à vous se donne.
> Recevés cest honneur, de qui le renom beau,
> Vivans, vous tirera de l'oublieux tombeau.
> Embrassés, fortunés, la despouille plus riche
> De cent riches pays que vous mettrés en friche.

> Faites que, revenans chez vous quelque matin,
> Vous vous trouviés chargés d'honneur et de butin.'
> Lors j'acheve et ma vois fut quant et quant suivie
> D'un frapement d'escus qui tesmoignoit l'envie
> Qu'ils avoyent de marcher sous mes fiers estandars.

['Avenge the greatest god who has descended from the starry circles. Arm, soldiers, arm, one hand with a torch, the other with a blade, to despoil the Occident by sword and by flame. Cover its mountains and valleys with a red sea. Make your proud horses swim in blood. Receive, happy, the sceptre and the crown of this great universe, which gives itself wholly to you. Receive that honour whose glorious renown shall draw you living from the forgetful tomb. Embrace, fortunate ones, the richest spoil of a hundred rich countries that you shall lay waste.' Thus I finished, and my voice was at once followed by a beating of shields, which witnessed the desire they had to march under my bold banners.]   (ed. Baïche, 1971, V.451–67)

Accordingly, in Du Bartas's recreation the terrified nations hasten to submit themselves not, as in the Book of Judith, to Nabuchodonosor as represented by Holofernes, but to Holofernes himself, a virtual self-made divinity:

> 'Nous ne venons icy', disent-ils, 'avec armes
> Pour resister au choc de tes braves gendarmes;
> Ains, prince, nous venons pour recevoir de toy
> Ou la vie ou mort; bref, telle quelle loy
> Qu'il te plaira donner. Tiennes sons nos campaignes,
> Tiennes sont nos cités, tiennes sont nos montaignes,
> Tiens sont nos gras troupeaux, tien est nostre thresor,
> Tiens sont nos beaux enfans, tiens sommes-nous encor.
> Il reste seulement que, bening, il te plaise
> Nous accepter pour tels. Hé, Dieu! quel plus grand aise,
> Hé, Dieu! quel plus grand heur nous pourroit advenir
> Que d'avoir un tel chef qui sçache soutenir
> Et la vaillante lance et la balance esgale
> Et qui par ses vertus les plus grands dieux esgale?'

['We come not here', they said, 'with arms to resist the assault of your brave warriors, but we come, prince, to receive from you life or death, in brief, whatever law it shall please you to give. Yours are our fields, yours are our cities, yours are our mountains, yours are our fat flocks, yours is our treasure, yours are our beautiful children, yours are our very selves. It remains only that, in your benignity, it may please you to accept us as such. O God, what greater ease, O God, what greater happiness could come upon us than to have such a leader who knows how to wield both the valiant lance and the scales of justice, and who by his virtues equals the greatest gods?'] (ed. Baïche, 1971, V.537–50)

On the one hand, the metaphysical stakes in Du Bartas, as well as the evocation of Holofernes' means and (would-be) ends, strikingly anticipate Marlowe. On the other, Tamburlaine's effective usurpation of the higher power whose 'scourge' he purports to be is hardly a feature of the recognized sources. When Mexía (1580, 1: 146, 267) recounts Tamburlaine's claim to incarnate the wrath of God, the conventional Christian framework supports the commonplace larger moral about tyrants divinely licensed for a time but ineluctably doomed – including, incidentally, Nabuchodonosor. Fortescue (1571, fols. 42ᵛ–44ʳ, 86ʳ) actually strengthens the point – 'la punition perpetuelle de l'autre vie' (Mexía 1580, 1: 147) becomes frankly 'Hell and damnation' (Fortescue 1571, fol. 43ʳ) – while the same eschatological assumptions naturally figure also in Whetstone (1586, p. 82).

Holofernes' florid recital of his conquests bears particular comparison with Tamburlaine's résumé of his career as it comes to a close – as Holofernes' own, ironically, is likewise about to do:

>   ... je gaigne ce mont dont les obliques cornes
> Fendent toute l'Asie et qui servent de bornes
> A meint puissant empire: où j'occis, je romps, j'ards
> Tout ce que je rencontre et mes felons soldars
> Font comme les faucheurs, qui d'une main adroitte
> Ne laissent apres eux une seule herbe droitte;
> [...]
>   L'Asie mise en friche et r'entrant au Levant,
> Je conqueste Coelé, sans pitié je ravage
> De l'Euphrate profond le plantureux rivage.
> Je deserte Rapses et l'Agraee abatu
> De ma puissante main recongoist la vertu.
>   De-là, tousjours suyvant le bord de la marine,
> Je gaste Madian, puis au nort m'achemine
> Vers le double Liban; je fourrage Damas
> Et ses villes Gaane, Abile et Hippe abas
> Et de là, curieux, je viens mes pas conduire
> Sur le mont d'où l'on voit Phoebus de nuict reluire
> Et se lever hatif, faisant marcher mon ost
> Vers l'Occident batu de phoenicée flot.

[... I gain that mountain whose oblique horns divide all Asia and which serve as the boundary for many a potent empire. There I slaughter, I smash, I burn all that I encounter, and my brutal soldiers behave like mowers and with an able hand leave no single blade of grass standing upright after them. . . . Asia laid to waste, and returning to the east, I conquer Coele; without pity I ravage the fertile banks of the deep Euphrates. I devastate Rapsis, and the land of the Agraei, beaten down, recognizes the power of my mighty hand.

Then, always following the shore-line, I spoil Midian, then make my way north to the double Lebanon; I ravage the region of Damascus and flatten its cities Gaane, Abila, and Hippas, and from there, curious, I direct my steps to that mountain whence one sees Phoebus emerge from night and rise abruptly, causing my host to march towards the west pounded by the waves of the Phoenician sea.] (ed. Baïche, 1971, V.473–532)

He may as well be tracing his route on a map, as Tamburlaine actually does, and he has some of the same imaginative distance on his exploits, as if conquest were modulating into exploration, even abstract intellectual endeavour. In Tamburlaine's case, this tendency carries so far as to make him a visionary booster of the global economy:

> Here I began to march towards Persia,
> Along Armenia and the Caspian Sea,
> And thence unto Bithynia, where I took
> The Turk and his great empress prisoners.
> Then marched I into Egypt and Arabia,
> And here, not far from Alexandria,
> Whereas the Terrene and the Red Sea meet,
> Being distant less than full a hundred leagues,
> I meant to cut a channel to them both
> That men might quickly sail to India.
> From thence to Nubia near Borno lake,
> And so along the Ethiopian sea,
> Cutting the tropic line of Capricorn,
> I conquered all as far as Zanzibar.
> Then, by the northern part of Africa,
> I came at last to Graecia, and from thence
> To Asia, where I stay against my will;
> Which is from Scythia, where I first began,
> Backward and forwards near five thousand leagues.
> (II, V.iii.126–44)

At the end, Tamburlaine, too, looks towards the west to lands beyond his reach:

> Look here, my boys, see what a world of ground
> Lies westward from the midst of Cancer's line
> Unto the rising of this earthly globe,
> Whereas the sun, declining from our sight,
> Begins the days with our antipodes.
> (145–49)

It may not be mere coincidence that Du Bartas's conqueror concludes his recital 'prez du rampart scythique [near the Scythian rampart]' (ed. Baïche, 1971, V.570), from which he has indeed moved 'backward and forwards' – in time and imagined space – since the opening of Book II ('Holoferne deja dans le rampart scythique / Plantoit ses estandars [Holofernes already set up his banners on the Scythian rampart]' [II.1–2]). The underlying biblical reference, of course, cannot be to Tamburlaine's homeland of Scythia; Du Bartas himself may have been puzzled, and Hudson did nothing to clarify the point. (His 'Scythique rampier' [ed. Craigie, 1941, II.1, V.580] represents the cowardly translator's way out *par excellence*.) In fact, as the more learned translators of the Authorized Version accurately established (Judith 3:10), Holofernes' camp is near 'Scythopolis', or Bethshan, on the West Bank of the Jordan – thus, a natural staging point for his invasion. But what Marlowe would have read in the Geneva Bible might well have strengthened – and perhaps all the more strongly because geographically, materially, he knew better – an imaginative association with Tamburlaine: specified there is 'a citie of the Scythians'.[36]

X

In staging a conqueror threatened with conquest by his captive, *Tamburlaine*, pioneering text though it was, had at least one notable precursor in Lyly's *Campaspe*, and if the latter play chose to register generically in the lightweight division, an intertextual evocation of Alexander in relation to Tamburlaine is not necessarily beside the point. That earlier conqueror's career had a fair amount in common with Tamburlaine's, from '[riding] in triumph through Persepolis' (I, II.v.50, 54) – the idea that thrills the Scythian with royal ambition at the outset – to doing so in Babylon, his final conquest. Indeed, Tamburlaine savours that culmination as a triumph over mortality itself, a literal overriding of Alexandrian and Assyrian accomplishment – and of femininity as well:

> Where Belus, Ninus, and great Alexander
> Have rode in triumph, triumphs Tamburlaine,
> Whose chariot wheels have burst th'Assyrians' bones,
> Drawn with these kings on heaps of carcasses.
> Now in the place where fair Semiramis,
> Courted by kings and peers of Asia,
> Hath trod the measures, do my soldiers march;
> And in the streets, where brave Assyrian dames
> Have rid in pomp like rich Saturnia,
> With furious words and frowning visages
> My horsemen brandish their unruly blades.
>   (II, V.i.69–79)

Yet for Tamburlaine thus to arrogate a bird's-eye view of Alexander – in effect, the historian's perspective – inevitably opens the door to irony at his expense. In particular, an audience might recall the perspective of Mexía, who admiringly yet coolly takes the measure of both conquerors together in a comment omitted from Whetstone's adaptation of the passage: 'il ne fut moind[r]e qu'Alexandre, ou s'il le fut, c'estoit bien peu [he was no lesser than Alexander, or if so, it was by very little]' (Mexía 1580, 1: 262).[37] Tamburlaine is about to learn that, in the Dance of Death, he will not always get to lead.

This irony, too, is more forcefully evoked by Mexía than by Whetstone. The latter, having established Tamburlaine as God's instrument for scourging the powerful, simply brings his career to a matter-of-fact halt – 'rather abruptly', as Cunningham observes (1981, p. 12): 'In the ende this great personage, without disgrace of fortune, after sundry great victories, by the course of nature died, and left behind him two sons, every way far unlike their father. . . .' (Whetstone 1586, p. 82). This dry narrative severely abridges the sumptuous evocation by Mexía (followed by Fortescue) of the great destroyer's culminating triumph as, paradoxically, one of civilization and creation. Mexía's effect comes far closer to Marlowe's, juxtaposing the sense of infinite possibility with the banal triumph of death:

> Ces choses accomplies, & ayant ce grand personnage conquis de grans pays, vaincu, & mis à mort plusieurs Rois, & grands seigneurs, ne trouvant aucune resistence en toute l'Asie, se retira en son pays chargé d'infinies richesses, & de la compagnie des principaux de tous les pays par luy suppeditez, lesquels apportoyent quant & [sic] eux la meilleure part de leurs biens: & là fit edifier vne fort magnifique ville, . . . la plus somptueuse ville du monde . . . abondante & pleine de toutes richesses. Mais enfin ce Tamburlam, combien qu'il maintint son estat en ceste grande authorité, si est-ce que comme homme, il paya le deuoir de nature, & fini ses iours laissant deux fils, non toutefois tels que leur pere. . . .

> [These things accomplished, and when this great personage had conquered many countries, vanquished, and put to death a number of kings, not finding any resistance in all of Asia, he withdrew into his country laden with infinite riches and accompanied by the principal persons of those lands that he had trodden underfoot, which persons carried with them the greater part of their goods. And there he caused a truly magnificent town to be constructed, . . . the most sumptuous city in the world . . . abounding and teeming with all riches. But at last this Tamburlaine, as much as he maintained his estate in great authority, yet so it was that, as a man, he paid the debt of nature and finished his days, leaving two sons, not, however, like their father . . .] (Mexía 1580, 1: 267–68)

Marlowe has offered previous intimations of this discrepant ending, one of which takes on particular irony in light of the source: his Tamburlaine kills a third son precisely for not being like him. But more sustained commentary comes through the playwright's principal innovation. The oversized hero waltzes through the better part of Part II with Zenocrate's corpse, in ostentatious but futile (and at least imaginatively malodorous) defiance of death's power to 'scourge the scourge of the immortal God' (II, II.iv.80). The grotesque futility of his continued possession of Zenocrate, however, echoes its remarkably complete realization in Part I.

That possession is complete, in fact, to the point where the numinous sense of the term suggests itself, with Zenocrate resembling Desdemona as seen through the lens of Brabantio. There is surely more involved than the positioning of a 'silenced woman on the margins of a formed male-male relationship', as Shepherd (1986, p. 203) puts it (with regard to the instantaneous bonding of Tamburlaine and Theridamus). Not only is Zenocrate actively enlisted in Tamburlaine's cause, but she occupies centre stage to a surprising degree, given the competing geopolitical events – from her introduction as a captive in Act I, Scene ii, to the marriage anticipated in the concluding lines. Fashioning himself as a Holofernes untouchable by any higher power, and so able to call all such power into question, requires fashioning her as a Judith figure with some precision, as an audience would arguably have appreciated. Only thus can the metaphysical magic of the Judith story – the Judith jinx – be enlisted in the Machiavellian cause.

For Tamburlaine, then, it is not enough to resist the female captive who threatens to captivate by her charms (as Alexander resists Campaspe),[38] to collect her as a trophy of victory (as Henry V does the Princess Katherine), or even to cultivate her complicity with 'custom-made persuasions' (Bartels 1993, p. 62), as he does with others. More profoundly, he must conjure and coopt Zenocrate's potential strength to act beyond the usual limits of her sex – to destroy him as a destroyer.[39] That strength is multiply established by presenting her as compassionate with the sufferings of others (especially her countrymen), devout, a dutiful daughter, and even finally, if momentarily, a virtual widow. (She thus fulfils the three estates of womanhood – as virgin-daughter, wife, and widow – elaborated at length by Du Bartas in establishing Judith's perfection [ed. Baïche, 1971, IV.73–239].) From the first, Tamburlaine's response is to take the conferring of her divinity into his own hands – rhetorically and otherwise: 'divine' becomes his insistent epithet for her. Despite her initial protest that 'The gods, defenders of the innocent, / Will never prosper your intended drifts' (I, I.ii.68–69), she becomes the gift of the same made-to-measure Jove who, if Theridamus should draw his sword 'to raze my charmèd skin', 'will stretch his hand from heaven / To ward the blow and shield me safe from harm' (178–80). The story of Judith is precisely inverted.

Yet even before she comes to pity the dead Bajazeth and his empress, Zenocrate willingly joins Tamburlaine in scorning them, and afterwards, when she prays, it is to ask 'mighty Jove and holy Mahomet' to 'Pardon my love' (V.i.364–65). If her dying fiancé leaves her 'wounded in conceit for thee, / As much as thy fair body is for me' (416–17), this hardly prevents her from jumping into Tamburlaine's arms ('Else should I much forget myself, my lord' [501]) or rejoicing as much as her father says he does in his own 'overthrow' (483). Her 'divinity', then, is not just the usual neo-platonic glamour but is teasingly enhanced by points of resemblance to Judith; and since the whole is entrusted to Tamburlaine's safe-keeping, his own godhead is the gainer. The culminating praise of the God of Israel proclaimed by the Judiths of the Bible and Du Bartas is recuperated by, and incorporated into, Tamburlaine's past and future triumphs:

> Then sit thou down, divine Zenocrate,
> And here we crown thee Queen of Persia
> And all the kingdoms and dominions
> That late the power of Tamburlaine subdued.
> As Juno, when the giants were suppressed
> That darted mountains at her brother Jove,
> So looks my love, shadowing in her brows
> Triumphs and trophies for my victories;
> Or as Latona's daughter bent to arms,
> Adding more courage to my conquering mind.
> (I, V.i.507–16)

As is signalled by the reference to Diana ('Latona's daughter'), what Tamburlaine most conspicuously keeps safe, despite his barbarous origins, is Zenocrate's chastity:

> Her state and person wants no pomp, you see,
> And for all blot of foul inchastity,
> I record heaven, her heavenly self is clear.
> Then let me find no further time to grace
> Her princely temples with the Persian crown.
> (V.i.486–90)

This declaration magnetically draws her father's blessing, too, within his hegemonic discourse: 'I yield with thanks and protestations / Of endless honour to thee for her love' (497–98).

In preserving the Soldan for this role while dispensing with the King of Arabia – indeed, in making the conquest of Egypt a resting point in the recreation of the world through destruction ('For Tamburlaine takes truce with all the world'

[V.i.530]) – Marlowe appears again to have seized an opportunity suggested by Mexía, followed by Fortescue, though not by Whetstone; behind the latter's bare statement that 'In Ægypt he encountred with the *Soudan*, and the King of *Arabia*, and ouerthrew them' (1586, p. 81) lies considerably more, including preparations to encounter Tamburlaine corresponding to Marlowe's Act IV, Scene iii:

> Puis paruenu en Egypte, le Soudan & le Roy d'Arabie, auec maintes autres prouinces s'assemblerent contre luy: mais venus à la bataille, ils furent mis en route, saccagez et vaincus, au moyen dequoy le Soudan se sauua par la fuitte: toutesfois le victorieux luy eust facilement osté l'Egypte, n'euste esté qu'il trouuoit tres-difficile chose de conduire par ces aspres deserts vne si puissante armee: pour ceste cause il differa de poursuyure d'auantage, & neantmoins subiugua le reste des parties limitrophes.

> [Then, once he was arrived in Egypt, the Sultan and the King of Arabia, with many other regions rallied against him. But when they came to the battle, they were routed, thrown into confusion and vanquished, with the result that the Sultan saved himself by flight. Nevertheless, the victor might easily have taken Egypt from him, were it not that he found it a very difficult matter to conduct such a strong army through those harsh deserts. For this reason he left off further pursuit, and nevertheless subjugated the rest of the contiguous territories.] (Mexía 1580, 1: 266)

Moreover, in stressing Tamburlaine's decision to '[take] truce with all the world', Marlowe appears to pick up the French version's 'il differa de poursuyure d'auantage', which clearly makes the halt to conquest a matter of choice. Fortescue's usually faithful translation omits this statement, instead presenting Tamburlaine – in most un-Marlovian fashion – as something close to daunted:

> How be it, *Tamburlaine* had easily taken from hym all *Egypte*, hadde it not been for the greate, and inaccessible, desertes in that country, through whiche to passe with so puisante an armie, was either impossible, or at the leaste verie difficill, notwithstandyng he subdued all suche partes of the Countrie as were next hym. (1571, fol. 85^v)

In terms of the biblical models of symbolic castration that hover in the background – Samson as well as Holofernes ('She that hath calmed the fury of my sword, / Which had ere this been bathed in streams of blood' [V.i.438–39]) – Tamburlaine's sexual self-restraint carries overtones of self-preservation. The model of Judith remains especially insistent. By respecting Zenocrate's chastity, he avoids the whirlpool of the Judith jinx, which caught hold of Holofernes by blinding his senses to the true nature and source of Judith's beauty.

For Tamburlaine to make Zenocrate his queen is to pre-empt the divine prerogative to designate her as the redemptress of her people, and this is all the easier to do because he has exterminated the greater part of her countrymen – and women. What is left of her people become his own, as her father survives to testify.

XI

In this context, Tamburlaine's moment of faltering before Zenocrate's beauty – hence his appreciation of 'beauty' itself (V.i.160), as enhanced by 'thy passion for thy country's love' (137) – emerges as a well-managed weak moment. His inward 'sufferings' (160) are ironically circumscribed between paroxysms of barbarity – his killing of the Damascan virgins and his taunting of Bajazeth – and they issue in a triumph over 'thoughts effeminate and faint' (177), accompanied by the Machiavellian affirmation that 'virtue solely is the sum of glory / And fashions men with true nobility' (189–90). That he is flirting with the Judith jinx would have been signalled for many spectators by the soliloquy's overlap with the almost equally lengthy one (both have roughly fifty lines) that Du Bartas, without biblical precedent, invents for his infatuated Holofernes, building it explicitly (in an anticipation of Lyly) on the same paradox of the captor captivated which points up the menace to Tamburlaine. The terms of the speeches are commonplace enough, but the contexts are not; nor are the spiritual resonances.

Unlike Tamburlaine, Holofernes is genuinely on the slippery slope to losing his manhood to a cluster of interrelated vices before he loses his life. But the contrast with Tamburlaine is also visible along the axis of 'virtue':

> 'Helas! helas!', dit-il, 'faut-il donc que je vive,
> O change malheureux! captif de ma captive?
> Mais est-ce vivre, helas! quand le corps abatu
> Et quand l'ame abrutie ont perdu leur vertu?
> [...]
>   Que me sert-il d'avoir maint prince surmonté,
> [...]
> Puis que je suis vaincu par le foible pouvoir
> D'une esclave Judit...?'

['Alas, alas', he said, must I then live – O miserable change – the captive of my captive? But is it to live, alas, when the body, stricken down, and the bewildered soul have lost their virtue?... What does it serve me to have overcome many a prince,... since I have been vanquished by the feeble power of Judith, a slave...?']   (ed. Baïche, 1971, V.41–56)

While Tamburlaine laments that Zenocrate's 'sorrows'(V.i.155), expressed by her beautifully 'flowing eyes'(146), 'lay more siege unto my soul / Than all my army to Damascus' walls' (155–56), he is not about to give in. For Holofernes, the battle is lost: 'le traict aigu qui de son bel œil part / Fauçant fer et soldats, m'outre de part en part [the sharp dart that flies from her beautiful eye, striking down sword and soldiers, bewilders me to the core]' (ed. Baïche, 1971, V.59–60). Tamburlaine's very pain affirms his discursive mastery – 'What is beauty, saith my sufferings, then?' (V.i.160); Judith's beauty renders Holofernes timid, blind and mute:

> Car je respecte tant les graces que les cieux,
> Prodigues, ont versé sur elle que mes yeux
> Ne l'osent regarder et ma langue s'atache
> A mon palais muet tout soudain qu'elle tasche
> Decouvrir ma douleur.

[For I so respect those graces that the heavens, prodigal, have poured upon her that my eyes do not dare look at her and my tongue suddenly clings mute to my palate when it tries to reveal my pain.] (ed. Baïche, 1971, V.83–87)

The moment that strips Holofernes of boldness ('Ne l'osent . . .') and compels his recognition of 'les cieux' shows him trapped in quicksand: an especially grotesque irony anticipates the fate of his tongue, 'qui souloit mesme outrager les cieux' (VI.221). Tamburlaine will nimbly talk his way out of danger and continue 'daring God out of heaven'.

Holofernes' moment of self-mocking surrender of his strength ironically heralds the triumph of Truth by way of Beauty: 'Changés doncques, Hebrieux, changés en ris vos larmes, / Triomphés de mon ost, de moy et de mes armes [Change, then, Hebrews, change your tears to laughter; triumph over my army, myself, and my arms]' (V.65–66). Against this background, the originality of Marlowe is to enforce the separation of Beauty from Truth, indeed, to defer the latter indefinitely. It is an irony not likely to have been lost on contemporary audiences that, when faced with Tamburlaine's superheated vitality, the 'three score thousand' (II, III.v.33) Hebrew warriors marshalled against him by the (Turkish) King of Jerusalem blend into the ethnic melting pot with the rest of the losers.

Notes

1 As it happens, Monluc's *Commentaires* constitute a relatively rare instance of a French book on a subject other than morality or religion demonstrably present in early modern England: a copy is recorded as being in the library of Sir Roger Townshend (Fehrenbach and Leedham-Green [eds] 1992–95, 1: 109 [No. 3.143]).

Staging the Judith jinx: heads or tales? 93

2 Street 1983, pp. 52 and 54–55.
3 Cited De Somogyi 1998, p. 156.
4 See Fronton Du Duc, trans. Hillman, 2000, Introd., pp. 43–51.
5 Bouzy's own seduction by the myth is suggested by his supposition that Judith actually had sex with Holofernes.
6 See Hillman 1997, pp. 165–66.
7 See Judg. 16:4–20.
8 De Somogyi's discussion of Parolles in this light is particularly convincing; he observes in passing (as others have done) Othello's 'odd resemblance to the *commedia* Capitano', given that Iago's 'poisonous lies . . . instigate the play's tragic catastrophe' (1998, p. 179).
9 See, most notably, Sokol 1991, pp. 131–35.
10 Cf. De Somogyi 1998, pp. 156–57, one of the few critics to find significance in the biblical origin of the character's name.
11 Shaheen 1999, p. 798, detects only five references to the Book of Judith in Shakespeare's œuvre (in *3H6, KJ, 2H4* and *H5*).
12 See Judith 14:10: 'And Achior, seeing all things that God had done for Israel, beleued in God vnfainedly, and circumcised the foreskine of his flesh, and was joyned vnto the house of Israel vnto this day.' Given the symbolic relation between decapitation and circumcision, it is remarkable that neither Freud himself nor his revisionist critics seem to have taken the latter element of the story of Judith into account. See Jacobus 1986, pp. 110–36.
13 See Holstein 1967, p. 20. German theatrical tradition assimilated Holofernes to a Turkish tyrant, Judith to Christianity, in line with Othello's suicidal conclusion.
14 Sylvester's translation was entitled *Bethulia's Rescue*; his complete folio collections of Du Bartas's works reprinted Hudson's version as well as his own in 1621, 1633 and 1641. On the bibliography, see Craigie (ed.) 1941, pp. xliii–xlvi.
15 Apart from the problematic relative authority of the Quarto and Folio texts, the most telling argument against reading 'Iudean' has been the strained quality of a reference to Judas and the remoteness of any other candidate proposed for the allusion (such as Herod, the killer of his wife Mariam). See Honigmann (ed.) 1997, p. 343, longer note to V.ii.345; Shaheen 1999, pp. 600–1; and Noble 1979, p. 273.
16 Isabella is also the name of the narrator of the analogous story in George Whetstone's *Heptameron*. Ariosto's treatment, however, would have rendered it especially suitable for Shakespeare's purposes, since God himself there decrees, following the heroine's death as a martyr to chastity, the name's eternal association with womanly purity, which writers will perpetuate (Canto 29, Stanza 29).
17 Cunningham (ed.) 1981, p. 18.
18 The heroic ruse of Isabella for thwarting the barbarian's designs on her chastity exercised considerable imaginative appeal in sixteenth-century French literature with *histoire tragique* affinities. In the tale of Laurine in Claude de Taillemont's *Discours des champs faëz* of 1553 (ed. Arnould, 1991, pp. 258–70), the heroine arranges her own murder, under a false identity, by the barbarian's servant, who is instructed

to present the severed head to her would-be seducer; like Rodomonte, the latter is suitably stricken and constructs an elaborate tomb. When Marie de Gournay adapted Taillemont's novel in *Le promenoir de Monsieur de Montaigne* (1594), she decorously left the head on her heroine's deceptively murdered corpse but made the allusion to Isabella more explicit: the benediction/epitaph provided at the conclusion closely echoes Ariosto, Canto 29, Stanza 27. (See *Le promenoir de Monsieur de Montaigne*, ed. Arnould, 1996, p. 168; *The Promenade of Monsieur de Montaigne*, trans. Hillman and Quesnel, 2002, p. 67.) For a reading of the novels of Taillemont and Gournay as intertexts of *MND*, see Hillman 2004, 'Des Champs faëz de Claude de Taillemont au labyrinthe du *Songe* shakespearien'.

19 Ariosto, trans. Harington, 1591, p. 239. The work of Rich (1940), though outdated in approach, remains a solid guide to Harington's idiosyncratic (not to say erratic) adaptation.

20 Here Harington's appended commentary again proves pertinent, though in a more personal (not to say naive) way; he reinforces the point, and endorses the charge carried by the name, by relating the exemplary character of his own mother Isabella, citing an anonymous tribute (his own?):

> A body chast, a vertuous mind, a temperat toung, an humble hart,
> Secret and wise, faithfull and kind, true without guile,
>   milde without art,
> A frend to peace, a foe to strife, a spotlesse mayd,
>   a matchlesse wife. (1591, p. 239)

Such idealization is obviously the other side of the coin of the attacks on women Harington freely serves up elsewhere (cf. Rich 1940, pp. 108–36).

21 Bandello, *Certaine Tragicall Discourses*, Disc. 4; cited Bullough (ed.) 1957–75, 7: 261.

22 The element of remorse is essential to the quintessentially tragic quality of this event, according to Jean Vauquelin de La Fresnaye in *L'art poétique*: 'Comme quand Rodomont abusé par cautelle, / Meurtrit se repentant la pudique Isabelle [As when Rodomont, deceived by a stratagem, slays – and repents for it – the chaste Isabelle]' (ed. Pellissier, 1885, Bk. 3, ll. 159–60). Vauquelin's treatise was not published until 1605, but it seems to have been composed between 1574 and 1589 (Pellissier [ed.] 1885, pp. xxxv–xxxvi); any relation to Montreux's play remains tantalizingly indistinct.

23 See above Chapter 3, pp. 55–56. The effect is even starker in a dramatization of Henri III's assassination composed, in the aftermath of the civil wars and under the auspices of Henri IV, by Jacques de Fonteny (pub. 1600). In *Cléophon, tragédie conforme et semblable à celles que la France a veues durant les guerres civilles*, the reprehensible Palamnaise, representing Jacques Clément, justifies himself with a pointed analogy involving Judith, Holofernes and the rescue of Bethulia (1600, p. 25).

24 This is, of course, the famous attack by Robert Greene in *Perimedes the Blacksmith* (1588).

Staging the Judith jinx: heads or tales? 95

25 Gruget would have been by definition a sympathetic figure for English Protestants, as one-time secretary to Marguerite de Navarre and the editor in 1559 of her *Heptaméron* at the direction of her daughter, Jeanne d'Albret (Cazaux 1973, p. 195).
26 Especially interesting on the latter remain Ellis-Fermor (ed.) 1951, Introd., pp. 17–61 and 286–307; Seaton 1929; and Bakeless 1964, 1: 204–38. Seaton, incidentally, proposes various French sources, including Belleforest's *Cosmographie universelle* (1575) – the latter also for *The Jew of Malta*; for his part, Bakeless particularly downplays Mexía, as well as Petrus Perondinus (see below, p. 79); neither Seaton nor Bakeless mentions Gruget.
27 Pt. 1, Ch. 32 (fol. 97ᵛ–99ʳ), in Mexía, *Les Diverses leçons de Pierre Messie, augmentées du quatriesme livre*, trans. Gruget (Paris: V. Sertenas, 1556); Pt. 1, Ch. 32 (1: 145–47), in *Les diverses leçons de Pierre Messie . . . Augmentées outre les precedentes impressions de la suite d' icelles, faite par Antoine du Verdier, Sieur de Vauprivaz . . .*, trans. (of Mexía) Gruget, 2 vols in 1 (Lyons: Estienne Michel, 1580); Pt. 1, Ch. 15, in Fortescue 1571, fols. 42ᵛ–44ʳ. For reasons of clarity and convenience, Fortescue's translation is cited under his own name from its first edition (1571), while subsequent references to the combined works of Gruget and Du Verdier cite (as 'Mexía 1580') the edition published in Lyons by Estienne Michel in that year.
28 Pt. 1, Ch. 13, in Mexía 1556 and 1580; Bk. 1, Ch. 11, in Whetstone 1586, pp. 69–78. The absence of this account from Fortescue provides the strongest evidence in favour of Whetstone adduced by Izard 1943, pp. 412–13.
29 Thus Izard concludes: 'The assumption that Marlowe used Whetstone eliminates the necessity of examining a number of related accounts'; in particular, 'Gruget (whom both Fortescue and Whetstone were translating) . . . may be omitted' (1943, p. 416). And so he is, even by critics whose concern with representation of the 'other' imposes a reexamination of sources; see notably Bartels 1993, pp. 57–59, 187–88n.17.
30 See Cunningham (ed.) 1981, pp. 10, 14, 324–26.
31 See (or rather hear) Pistol in *2H4*:

> Shall packhorses
> And hollow pamper'd jades of Asia,
> Which cannot go but thirty mile a day,
> Compare with Caesars and with Cannibals
> And Troiant Greeks? Nay, rather damn them with
> King Cerberus, and let the welkin roar.
> (II.iv.163–68)

Cf. *Tamburlaine, Part Two*:

> Holla, ye pampered jades of Asia!
> What, can ye draw but twenty miles a day,
> And have so proud a chariot at your heels,
> And such a coachman as great Tamburlaine . . . ?
> (IV.iii.1–4)

32 See Seaton 1924, pp. 13–35, and 1929, pp. 389–90; Bakeless 1942, 1: 236–37.

33 Arguably, however, this is one of the few points where that generally straightforward dramatization of David's uneasy relations with God receives a secular inflection; the bare biblical report of Joab that he has 'taken the city of waters' (2 Sam. 12:27) is rendered more explicit by Peele ('The conduit heads and all their sweetest springs' [ed. Blistein, 1970, 230]), while the lines cited by De Somogyi are actually an addition establishing this as a deliberate tactic, proposed by Urias: 'Let us assault and scale this kingly Tower, / Where all their conduits and the fountaines are, / Then we may easily take the citie too' (1998, 180–82).

34 Cf. Hudson's introductory summary of Book III: '... *the Poet setteth forth the seege of Bethulia, and the extremitie that God permitted them to feele, thereby to give an entrie to his miraculous deliverance: who is accustomed to lead his people to the gates of death, and from thence to retyre them aboue all humaine expectation, to the end they should confesse that the arme of of flesh, nor worldly wisedom mainteines not the Church: but the onelie favour of the Almightie to whome, the whole glorie of duetie should be rendred.*' (Craigie [ed.] 1941, p. 41 [ll. 1–10]).

35 The 'curtle-axe' (the word derives from 'coutelas' – see OED), is also Tamburlaine's characteristic weapon: 'See where it is, the keenest curtleaxe / That e'er made passage thorough Persian arms' (I, II.iii.55–56).

36 In fact, the name Scythopolis may be the trace of an ancient Scythian invasion; the Greek name is first documented from the Books of Judith and Maccabees (II Mach. 12:29) – see Herbermann *et al.* (eds), www.newadvent.org/cathen/, *The Catholic Encyclopedia*, s.v. Scythopolis – so the confusion on the part of early readers is understandable.

37 Cf. Whetstone 1586, p. 79, where, moreover, Mexía's praise of Tamburlaine's quickness, aptness, and heroic aspiration – points taken up by Marlowe – is condensed and toned down.

38 'What, is the son of Philip, King of Macedon, become the subject of Campaspe, the captive of Thebes?' (Lyly, ed. Hunter, 1991, II.ii.35–36). The places where Lyly might have found the story of Alexander, Campaspe and Apelles similarly moralized include Mexía 1580, 1: 230–35 (Pt. 2, Ch. 17), though there she is unequivocally Alexander's 'concubine', as Fortescue signals in a marginal note to his translation (1971, fol. 68ʳ).

39 Cf. Cartwright 1999, pp. 213–17.

Works cited

Early texts and editions

Ariosto, Lodovico. *Orlando Furioso*, 2 vols. Ed. Lanfranco Caretti. Introd. Italo Calvino. Turin: Einaudi, 1966.
___. *Orlando furioso in English heroical verse.* Trans. John Harington. London: Richard Field, 1591.
Aubigné, Agrippa d'. *Les tragiques.* Ed. Frank Lestringant. Paris: Gallimard, 1995.
Beaumont, Francis. *The Knight of the Burning Pestle.* Ed. Sheldon P. Zitner. The Revels Plays. Manchester: Manchester University Press, 1984.
Belyard, Simon. *Le Guysien ou perfidie tyrannique commise par Henry de Valois es personnes des illustriss. reverdiss. & tresgenereux Princes Loys de Loraine Cardinal & Archeuesque de Rheims, & Henry de Loraine Duc de Guyse, grand Maistre de France.* Troyes: Jean Moreau, 1592.
Bevington, David (ed.). *Medieval Drama.* Boston: Houghton Mifflin, 1975.
Bèze, Théodore de (attrib.). *Histoire ecclésiastique des églises réformées du Royaume de France*, 3 vols. Ed. G. Baum and E. Cunitz. 1883–89; rpt. Nieuwkoop: B. De Graaf, 1974.
The Bible and Holy Scriptvres Conteyned in the Olde and Newe Testament. Geneva: [n.pub.], 1562 [i.e. 1561]. STC 2095.
Billard de Courgenay, Claude. *La mort d'Henri IV, tragédie en 5 actes et en vers.* 1610. Paris: Léopold Collin, 1806.
Brantôme, Pierre de Bourdeille, abbé de. *Œuvres complètes,* 11 vols. Ed. Ludovic Lalanne. Paris: La Société de l'Histoire de France, 1864–82.
Bullough, Geoffrey (ed.). *Narrative and Dramatic Sources of Shakespeare,* 8 vols. London: Routledge; New York: Columbia University Press, 1957–75.
Chantelouve, François de. *La tragédie de feu Gaspard de Coligny.* Ed. Keith Cameron. Exeter: University of Exeter Press, 1971.
___. *The Tragedy of the Late Gaspard de Coligny. The Tragedy of the Late Gaspard de Coligny and The Guisiade* [by Pierre Matthieu]. Trans. with Introduction and Notes by Richard Hillman. Carleton Renaissance Plays in Translation, 40. Ottawa: Dovehouse Editions, 2005.

Claudian [Claudian Claudianus]. *In Rufinum [Against Rufinus]. Claudian*, 2 vols. Ed. Maurice Platnauer. Loeb Classical Library. Cambridge, MA: Harvard University Press; London: Heinemann, 1976. Vol. 1.

Daniel, Samuel. *The First Fowre Bookes of the Civile Wars. Narrative and Dramatic Sources of Shakespeare*, vol. 3. Ed. Geoffrey Bullough. London: Routledge; New York: Columbia University Press, 1960. 434–60.

Donne, John. *Devotions upon Emergent Occasions, together with Death's Duel*. Ann Arbor: University of Michigan Press, 1959.

Drummond, William. *Conversations with William Drummond of Hawthornden. Ben Jonson*. Ed. Ian Donaldson. The Oxford Authors. Oxford: Oxford University Press, 1985. 595–611.

Du Bartas, Guillaume de Salluste, seigneur. *La Judit*. Ed. André Baïche. Publications de la Faculté des Lettres et Sciences Humaines de Toulouse, ser. A, vol. 12. Toulouse: Association des Publications de la Faculté des Lettres et Sciences Humaines de Toulouse, 1971.

____. *Thomas Hudson's Historie of Judith*. Trans. Thomas Hudson. Ed. James Craigie. Edinburgh: William Blackwood and Sons, 1941.

Du Rosier, Pierre. *Déploration de la France sur la calamité des dernieres guerres ciuilles aduenues en icelle, l'an 1568*. Paris: Denis du Pré, 1568.

Fleury, Antoine. *Responce à un certain escrit, publié par l'Admiral & ses adherans, prentendans couvrir & excuser la rupture qu'ils ont faite de l'Edict de Pacification, & leurs nouveaux remuemens & entreprinses contre l'Estat du Roi, & le bien & repos de ses subjectz*. Paris: Claude Frémy, 1568.

Fonteny, Jacques de. *Cléophon, tragédie conforme et semblable à celles que la France a veues durant les guerres civilles*. Paris: F. Jacquin, 1600.

Fortescue, George. *The Foreste, or Collection of Histories*. London: John Kingston for William Jones, 1571. STC 17849.

Fronton Du Duc. *L'histoire tragique de la Pucelle de Dom-Rémy*. Ed. Marc André Prévost. *La tragédie à l'époque d'Henri III*, vol. 2 (1579–82). Théâtre français de la Renaissance, 2nd ser. Florence: Leo S. Olschki; Paris: Presses Universitaires de France, 2000.

____. *The Tragic History of the Pucelle of Domrémy, Otherwise Known as the Maid of Orléans*. Trans. with Introduction and Notes by Richard Hillman. Carleton Renaissance Plays in Translation, 39. Ottawa: Dovehouse Editions, 2005.

Garnier, Robert. *Cornelia*. Trans. Thomas Kyd. *The Works of Thomas Kyd*. Ed. Frederick S. Boas. Oxford: Clarendon Press, 1901.

____. *Cornélie*. Ed. Jean-Claude Ternaux. Textes de la Renaissance. Paris: H. Champion, 2002.

____. *Porcie*. Ed. Raymond Lebègue. *Œuvres complètes de Robert Garnier. Porcie, Cornélie*. Les Textes Français. Paris: Les Belles Lettres, 1973.

____. *Porcie, tragédie françoise, représentant la cruelle et sanglante saison des guerres civiles de Rome, propre et convenable pour y voir dépeincte la calamité de ce temps*. Paris: R. Estienne, 1568.

Works cited

Gibbon, Charles. *A watch-worde for warre. Not so new as necessary, etc.* [London]: [J. Roberts for] John Legat, 1596. STC 11492.

Goulart, Simon (attrib.); Jean de Serres (attrib.); Pierre Matthieu, et al. *Histoire des choses mémorables avenues en France, depuis l'an 1547 jusques au commencement de l'an 1597, sous le règne de Henri II, François II, Charles IX, Henri III et Henri IV, contenant infinies merveilles de notre siècle. Dernière édition.* [n.p.]: [n.pub.], 1599.

____ (attrib.); Jean de Serres (attrib.); Pierre Matthieu, et al. *An historical collection, of the most memorable accidents, and tragicall massacres of France, vnder the raignes of Henry. 2. Francis. 2. Charles. 9. Henry. 3. Henry. 4. now liuing.* Trans. anon. London: Thomas Creede, 1598. STC 11275.

Gournay, Marie le Jars de. *The Promenade of Monsieur de Montaigne.* Ed. and trans. Richard Hillman and Colette Quesnel. Introd. Richard Hillman. *Apology for the Woman Writing and Other Works.* The Other Voice in Early Modern Europe. Chicago: University of Chicago Press, 2002. 27–67.

____. *Le promenoir de Monsieur de Montaigne. Texte de 1641, avec les variantes des éditions de 1594, 1595, 1598, 1599, 1607, 1623, 1626, 1627, 1634.* Ed. Jean-Claude Arnould. Études Montaignistes, 26. Paris: H. Champion, 1996.

Grévin, Jacques. *César.* Ed. Ellen S. Ginsberg. Textes littéraires français. Geneva: Droz; Paris: Minard, 1971.

Hotman, François. *La Gavle Françoise de François Hotoman* [sic] *Jurisconsulte. Nouuellement traduite de Latin en François.* Trans. Simon Goulart. Cologne: Hierome Bertulphe, 1574.

Hurault, Michel, seigneur Du Fay. *A discourse vpon the present estate of France. Togither with a copie of the kings letters patents, declaring his mind after his departure out of Paris. Whereunto is added the copie of two letters written by the Duke of Guize.* Trans. Edward Aggas. [London]: [John Wolfe], 1588. STC 14004.

____. *An excellent discourse vpon the now present estate of France.* Trans. E[dward] A[ggas]. London: John Wolfe, 1592. STC 14005.

____. *Excellent et libre discours, sur l'estat present de la France. Le troisiesme recveil, contenant les choses les plus memorables advenves sous la Ligue, tant en France, Angleterre, qu'autres lieux.* Ed. Simon Goulart. [n.p.]: [n.pub.], 1593. 2–55.

Jonson, Ben. *Ben Jonson*, 11 vols. Ed. C. H. Herford, Percy Simpson and Evelyn Simpson. Oxford: Clarendon Press, 1925–52.

____. *Sejanus His Fall.* Ed. Philip J. Ayres. The Revels Plays. Manchester: Manchester University Press, 1990.

____. *Volpone.* Ed. R. Brian Parker. The Revels Plays. Manchester: Manchester University Press, 1983.

Kyd, Thomas. *The Spanish Tragedy.* Ed. Philip Edwards. The Revels Plays. London: Methuen, 1959.

L'Estoile, Pierre de. *Registre-journal du règne de Henri III*, 6 vols. Ed. Madeleine Lazard and Gilbert Schrenck. Geneva: Droz, 1992–2003.

Lyly, John. *Campaspe. Campaspe, Sappho and Phao.* Ed. G. K. Hunter. The Revels Plays. Manchester: Manchester University Press, 1991.

Mareschal, André. *La cour bergère, ou L'Arcadie de Messire Philippe Sidney*. Paris: T. Quinet, 1640.
Marlowe, Christopher ('and his collaborator and revisers'). *Dr Faustus, A-text (1604)*. *Doctor Faustus, A- and B-texts (1606, 1616)*. Ed. David Bevington and Eric Rasmussen. The Revels Plays. Manchester: Manchester University Press, 1993.
———. *Edward the Second*. Ed. Charles R. Forker. The Revels Plays. Manchester: Manchester University Press, 1994.
———. *The Jew of Malta*. Ed. N. W. Bawcutt. The Revels Plays. Manchester: Manchester University Press; Baltimore, MD: Johns Hopkins University Press: 1978.
———. *The Massacre at Paris. Dido Queen of Carthage and The Massacre at Paris*. Ed. H. J. Oliver. The Revels Plays. London: Methuen, 1968.
———. *Tamburlaine the Great*. Ed. J. S. Cunningham. The Revels Plays. Manchester: Manchester University Press; Baltimore, MD: Johns Hopkins University Press, 1981.
———. *Tamburlaine the Great: In Two Parts*, 2nd edn. Ed. Una M. Ellis-Fermor. *The Works and Life of Christopher Marlowe*, gen. ed. R. H. Case. London: Methuen, 1951.
Marston, John. *Antonio's Revenge*. Ed. G. K. Hunter. Regents Renaissance Drama Series. Lincoln: University of Nebraska Press, 1965.
Matthieu, Pierre. *La Guisiade*. Ed. Louis Lobbes. Geneva: Droz, 1990.
———. *The Guisiade. The Tragedy of the Late Gaspard de Coligny* [by François de Chantelouve] *and The Guisiade*. Trans. with Introduction and Notes by Richard Hillman. Carleton Renaissance Plays in Translation, 40. Ottawa: Dovehouse Editions, 2005.
———. *Histoire des derniers troubles de France, sous les règnes des rois . . . Henry III . . . et Henri IIII*. Lyons: E. Bonaventure, 1596.
Mexía, Pedro. *Les diverses leçons de Pierre Messie, . . . contenans la lecture de variables histoires et autres choses mémorables, augmentées du quatriesme livre, le tout mis en françois par Claude Gruget*. Trans. Claude Gruget. Paris: V. Sertenas, 1556.
———. and Antoine Du Verdier. *Les diverses leçons de Pierre Messie gentil-homme de Seville . . . contenans variables et memorables histoires, . . . Augmentées outre les precedentes impressions de la suite d'icelles, faite par Antoine Du Verdier, Sieur de Vauprivaz, etc.*, 2 vols in 1. Trans. (of Mexía) Claude Gruget. Lyons: Estienne Michel, 1580.
Montaigne, Michel de. *Les Essais de Michel de Montaigne. Édition conforme au texte de l'exemplaire de Bordeaux avec les additions de l'édition posthume, l'explication des termes vieillis et la traduction des citations, une étude sur Montaigne, une chronologie de sa vie etc*, nouvelle edn. Ed. Pierre Villey. Rev. ed. V.-L. Saulnier. Paris: Presses Universitaires de France, 1965.
———. *Montaigne's Essays*. Trans. John Florio. Ed. L. C. Harmer. London: Dent; New York: Dutton, 1965.
Montreux, Nicolas de [pseud. 'Ollenix du Mont-Sacré']. *La tragédie d'Isabelle. Le Quatrième livre des Bergeries de Julliette . . . ensemble la tragédie d'Isabelle*. Paris: G. Des Rues, 1595.
Peele, George. *David and Bathsabe*. Ed. Elmer Blistein. *The Dramatic Works of George Peele. The Life and Works of George Peele*, 3 vols. New Haven, CT: Yale University Press, 1970. Vol. 3.

Works cited 101

Sackville, Thomas, and Thomas Norton. *Gorboduc, or Ferrex and Porrex*. *Drama of the English Renaissance, Vol. I: The Tudor Period*. Ed. Russell A. Fraser and Norman Rabkin. Upper Saddle River, NJ: Prentice-Hall, 1976.
Seneca, Lucius Annaeus. L. *Annaei Senecae Ad Lucilium Epistulae Morales*. Ed. L. D. Reynolds. Oxford: Clarendon Press, 1965.
Shakespeare, William. *Othello*. Ed. E. A. J. Honigmann. The Arden Shakespeare (3rd ser.). Walton-on-Thames, Surrey: Thomas Nelson and Sons, 1997.
___. *Richard II*. Ed. Charles R. Forker. The Arden Shakespeare (3rd ser.). London: Routledge, 2001.
___. *The Riverside Shakespeare*, 2nd edn. Gen. eds G. Blakemore Evans and J. J. M. Tobin. Boston: Houghton Mifflin, 1997.
Sidney, Philip. *An Apology for Poetry*. Ed. Geoffrey Shepherd. Manchester: Manchester University Press; New York: Barnes and Noble, 1973.
Spenser, Edmund. *The Complete Poetical Works of Spenser*. Ed. R. E. Neil Dodge. The Cambridge Edition of the Poets. Boston: Houghton Mifflin, 1908.
Taillemont, Claude de. *Discours des champs faëz. À l'honneur, et exaltation de l'Amour et des Dames (1553)*. Ed. Jean-Claude Arnould. Textes Littéraires Français. Geneva: Droz, 1991.
La tragédie française du bon Kanut, roi de Danemark. Ed. Christiane Lauvergnat-Gagnière. *La tragédie à l'époque d'Henri III*, vol. 1 (1574–79). Théâtre français de la Renaissance, 2nd ser. Florence: Leo S. Olschki; Paris: Presses Universitaires de France, 1999.
Vauquelin de La Fresnaye, Jean. *L'art poétique de Vauquelin de La Fresnaye: Où l'on peut remarquer la perfection et le défaut des anciennes et des modernes poésies. Texte conforme à l'éd. de 1605*. Ed. Georges Pellissier. Paris: Garnier, 1885.
Webster, John. *The Duchess of Malfi*. Ed. John Russell Brown. The Revels Plays. London: Methuen, 1964.
Whetstone, George. *The English Myrror*. London: J. Windet for G. Seton, 1586. STC 25336.
Woodstock: A Moral History. Ed. A. P. Rossiter. London: Chatto & Windus, 1946.

Critical and historical scholarship

Bakeless, John. *The Tragicall History of Christopher Marlowe*, 2 vols. 1942; rpt. Hamdon, CT: Archon, 1964.
Bartels, Emily C. *Spectacles of Strangeness: Imperialism, Alienation, and Marlowe*. Philadelphia: University of Pennsylvania Press, 1993.
Baschet, Armand. *Les comédiens italiens à la cour de France sous Charles IX, Henri III, Henri IV et Louis XIII: d'après les lettres royales, la correspondance originale des comédiens, les registres de la Trésorerie de l'épargne et autres documents*. Paris: E. Plon, 1882.
Biet, Christian. Introduction. *Théâtre de la cruauté et récits sanglants: en France (XVIe–XVIIe) siècles*. Ed. Christian Biet. Paris: Robert Laffont, 2006. v–xlvii.
Bourassin, Emmanuel. *L'Assassinat du duc de Guise*. Paris: Perrin, 1991.

Bouzy, Olivier. 'Images bibliques à l'origine de l'image de Jeanne d'Arc.' *Images de Jeanne d'Arc. Actes du Colloque de Rouen 25, 26, 27 mai 1999*. Ed. Jean Maurice and Daniel Couty. Paris: Presses Universitaires de France, 2000. 237–42.

Braden, Gordon. *Renaissance Tragedy and the Senecan Tradition: Anger's Privilege*. New Haven, CT: Yale University Press, 1985.

Cartwright, Kent. *Theatre and Humanism: English Drama in the Sixteenth Century*. Cambridge: Cambridge University Press, 1999.

Cazaux, Yves. *Jeanne d'Albret*. Paris: Éditions Albin Michel, 1973.

Chaintron, Maria. *Le duc d'Épernon 1554–1642. L'ascension prodigieuse d'un cadet de Gascogne*. Paris: Éditions Publisud, 1988.

Chaix, Paul, Alain Dufour and Gustave Moeckli. *Les livres imprimés à Genève de 1550 à 1600*, rev. edn. Travaux d'Humanisme et Renaissance, 86. Geneva: Droz, 1966.

Cox, John D. *The Devil and the Sacred in English Drama, 1350–1642*. Cambridge: Cambridge University Press, 2000.

Crouzet, Denis. *La genèse de la Réforme française, 1520–1562*. Paris: SEDES, 1996.

____. *Les guerriers de Dieu. La violence au temps des troubles de religion (vers 1525–vers 1610)*, 2 vols. Seyssel: Champ Vallon, 1990.

____. *La nuit de la Saint-Barthélemy. Un rêve perdu de la Renaissance*. Paris: Fayard, 1994.

Deierkauf-Holsboer, S. Wilma. *Le théâtre de l'Hôtel de Bourgogne, Vol. I: 1548–1635*. Paris: Nizet, 1968.

De Somogyi, Nick. *Shakespeare's Theatre of War*. Aldershot and Burlington, VT: Ashgate, 1998.

Fehrenbach, Robert J., and E. S. Leedham-Green (eds). *Private Libraries in Renaissance England: A Collection and Catalogue of Tudor and Early Stuart Book-Lists*, 4 vols. Medieval and Renaissance Texts and Studies. Binghamton, NY: MRTS; Marlborough: Adam Matthew, 1992–95.

Gibbons, Brian. 'Romance and the Heroic Play.' *The Cambridge Companion to English Renaissance Drama*. Ed. A. R. Braunmuller and Michael Hattaway. Cambridge: Cambridge University Press, 1990. 207–36.

Greenblatt, Stephen J. *Hamlet in Purgatory*. Princeton, NJ: Princeton University Press, 2001.

Herbermann, Charles G. et al. (eds). *The Catholic Encyclopedia*. www.newadvent.org/cathen/ (accessed January 2010).

Helgerson, Richard. *Forms of Nationhood: The Elizabethan Writing of England*. Chicago: University of Chicago Press, 1992.

Hillman, Richard. 'Des Champs faëz de Claude de Taillemont au labyrinthe du Songe shakespearien, en passant par le Proumenoir de Monsieur de Montaigne.' *Studi Francesi* 48.1 (2004): 3–18.

____. *French Reflections in the Shakespearean Tragic: Three Case Studies*. Manchester: Manchester University Press (forthcoming).

____. *Intertextuality and Romance in Renaissance Drama: The Staging of Nostalgia*. Basingstoke, Hampshire: Macmillan; New York: St Martin's Press, 1992.

____. 'Marlowe's Guise: Offending against God and King.' *Notes and Queries* 55.2 (2008): 154–59.

____. 'A Midsummer Night's Dream and La Diane of Nicolas de Montreux.' Review of English Studies 61 (2010): 34–54; doi: 10.1093/res/hgp030.

____. Self-Speaking in Medieval and Early Modern English Drama: Subjectivity, Discourse and the Stage. Basingstoke, Hampshire: Macmillan; New York: St Martin's Press, 1997.

____. Shakespeare, Marlowe and the Politics of France. Basingstoke, Hampshire: Palgrave, 2002.

____. 'The Tragic Channel-Crossings of George Chapman, Part I: Bussy D'Ambois and The Conspiracy and Tragedy of Byron.' Cahiers Élisabéthains 45 (2004): 25–43.

____. 'The Tragic Channel-Crossings of George Chapman, Part II: The Revenge of Bussy D'Ambois and The Tragedy of Chabot.' Cahiers Élisabéthains 47 (2005): 1–9.

Holstein, Hugo. Die Reformation im Spiegelbild der dramatischen Literatur des sechzehnten Jahrhunderts. Schriften des Vereins für Reformationsgeschichte, 14–15. 1886; rpt. Nieuwkoop: B. de Graaf, 1967.

Izard, Thomas C. 'The Principal Source for Marlowe's Tamburlaine.' Modern Language Notes 58 (1943): 411–17.

Jacobus, Mary. 'Judith, Holofernes and the Phallic Woman.' Reading Woman: Essays in Feminist Criticism. London: Methuen, 1986. 110–36.

Jones, Leonard Chester. Simon Goulart 1543–1628. Étude biographique et bibliographique. Geneva: Georg; Paris: H. Champion, 1917.

Jouanna, Arlette, Jacqueline Boucher, Dominique Biloghi et al. (eds). Histoire et dictionnaire des Guerres de Religion. Paris: Robert Laffont, 1998.

Kelley, Donald R. The Beginning of Ideology: Consciousness and Society in the French Reformation. Cambridge: Cambridge University Press, 1981.

Kibbee, Douglas A. For to Speke Frenche Trewely: The French Language in England, 1000–1600: Its Status, Description and Instruction. Amsterdam Studies in the Theory and History of Linguistic Science, ser. 3. Studies in the History of the Language Sciences, 60. Amsterdam: John Benjamins, 1991.

King, Ros. '"The Disciplines of War": Elizabethan War Manuals and Shakespeare's Tragicomic Vision.' Shakespeare and War. Ed. Ros King and Paul J. C. M. Franssen. Basingstoke, Hampshire: Palgrave Macmillan, 2008. 15–29.

Kingdon, Robert M. Myths about the St. Bartholomew's Day Massacres 1572–1576. Cambridge, MA: Harvard University Press, 1988.

Kocher, Paul H. 'Marlowe's Art of War.' Studies in Philology 39 (1942): 207–25.

Laroque, François. '"Bellona's Bridegroom": la fête de la guerre dans le théâtre de Shakespeare.' Shakespeare et la guerre. Société Française Shakespeare, Actes du Congrès 1989. Ed. M. T. Jones-Davies. Paris: Les Belles Lettres, 1990. 25–46.

Lawrence, Jason. 'Who the Devil Taught Thee So Much Italian?': Italian Language Learning and Literary Imitation in Early Modern England. Manchester: Manchester University Press, 2005.

Lazard, Madeleine. Le théâtre en France au XVIe siècle. Littératures Modernes. Paris: Presses Universitaires de France, 1980.

Macintire, Elizabeth Jelliffe. 'French Influence on the Beginnings of English Classicism.' PMLA 26 (1911): 496–527.

Miola, Robert S. *Shakespeare and Classical Tragedy: The Influence of Seneca*. Oxford: Oxford University Press, 1992.

Neill, Michael. *Putting History to the Question: Power, Politics, and Society in English Renaissance Drama*. New York: Columbia University Press, 2000.

Noble, Richmond. *Shakespeare's Biblical Knowledge and Use of the Book of Common Prayer, as Exemplified in the Plays of the First Folio*. 1935; rpt. New York: Octagon, 1970.

Patterson, Annabel. *Shakespeare and the Popular Voice*. Oxford: Blackwell, 1989.

Postel, Claude. *Traité des invectives au temps de la Réforme*. Paris: Les Belles Lettres, 2004.

Rich, Townsend. *Harington and Ariosto: A Study in Elizabethan Verse Translation*. Yale Studies in English, 92. New Haven, CT: Yale University Press, 1940.

Riffaterre, Michael. 'L'intertexte inconnu.' *Littérature* 41 (1981): 4–7.

____. 'Sémiotique intertextuelle: l'interprétant.' *Revue d'esthétiques* 1–2 (1979): 128–50.

____. 'Syllepsis.' *Critical Inquiry* 6 (1980): 625–38.

Rowse, A. L. *Christopher Marlowe: A Biography*, rev. edn. London: Macmillan, 1981.

Seaton, Ethel. 'Fresh Sources for Marlowe.' *Review of English Studies* 5 (1929): 385–401.

____. 'Marlowe's Map.' *Essays and Studies by Members of the English Association* 10 (1924): 13–35.

Shaheen, Naseeb. *Biblical References in Shakespeare's Plays*. Newark, DE: University of Delaware Press; London: Associated University Presses, 1999.

Shepard, Alan. *Marlowe's Soldiers: Rhetorics of Masculinity in the Age of the Armada*. Aldershot and Burlington, VT: Ashgate, 2002.

Shepherd, Simon. *Marlowe and the Politics of Elizabethan Theatre*. Brighton: Harvester, 1986.

Simonini, Rinaldo C. *Italian Scholarship in Renaissance England*. The University of North Carolina Studies in Comparative Literature, 3. Chapel Hill, NC: University of North Carolina Press, 1952.

Sokol, B. J. 'Holofernes in Rabelais and Shakespeare and Some Verses of Thomas Harriot.' *Études rabelaisiennes*, vol. 25. Travaux d'Humanisme et Renaissance, 253. Geneva: Droz, 1991. 131–35.

Street, J. S. *French Sacred Drama from Bèze to Corneille: Dramatic Forms and their Purposes in the Early Modern Theatre*. Cambridge: Cambridge University Press, 1983.

Weil, Judith. *Christopher Marlowe: Merlin's Prophet*. Cambridge: Cambridge University Press, 1977.

Yates, Frances. *John Florio: The Life of an Italian in Shakespeare's England*. 1934; rpt. New York: Octagon, 1968.

Index

Albret, Jeanne d' (Queen of Navarre) 63, 95n.25
Alençon, François-Hercule, Duke of (latterly Duke of Anjou) 59n.9
Angoulême, Marguerite d' (Queen of Navarre) *see* Marguerite de Navarre
Anjou, François-Hercule, Duke of *see* Alençon
Antonius, Marcus 11, 74
Arcadius (Emperor of the Eastern Roman Empire) 57
Arc, Jeanne d' *see* Jeanne d'Arc
Ariosto, Lodovico (*Orlando Furioso*) 75–77, 93n.16, 93–94n.18, 94n.19, 94n.20, 94n.22
Aubigné, Agrippa d' (*Les tragiques*) 61n.27
Augustus, C. Octavius (Emperor of Rome) 11
Ayres, Philip J. 60n.23, 61n.25, 61n.30

Baïche, André 61n.26, 61n.27
Baines, Richard 82
Bajazeth [Bayesid] I (Ottoman Sultan) 79
Bakeless, John 95n.26, 96n.32
Bandello, Matteo (*Certaine Tragicall Discourses*) 76, 94n.21
Barricades, Day of the (12 May 1588) 30
Bartels, Emily C. 88, 95n.29

Baschet, Armand 15n.18
Beaumont, Francis (*The Knight of the Burning Pestle*) 33
Belleforest, François de
    Cosmographie universelle 95n.26
    Histoires tragiques 40, 59n.9
Belyard, Simon (*Le Guysien*) 6
Bèze, Théodore de 47
    Histoire ecclésiastique des églises réformées du Royaume de France 61n.27
Bible, The 23–24, 34, 40, 49, 54, 60n.20, 63–75 *passim*, 77, 78, 79, 80–81, 82, 83, 86, 89, 90, 93n.7, 93n.10, 93n.11, 93n.12, 93n.13, 93n.15, 94n.23, 96n.33, 96n.36
Biet, Christian 13–14
Billard de Courgenay, Claude (*La mort d'Henri IV*) 50–51
Biloghi, Dominique 59n.9, 61n.27
Biron, Charles de Gontaut, Duke of 20, 21
Boucher, Jacqueline 59n.9, 61n.27
Bouillon, Godefroy [Godefroid] de 39
Bourassin, Emmanuel 60n.21
Bourbon, Antoine de (King of Navarre) 3–4
Bourbon, Henri I de *see* Condé
Bourdeille, Pierre de, abbé de Brantôme *see* Brantôme
Bouzy, Olivier 66, 93n.5
Braden, Gordon 58n.3, 58n.4

Brantôme, Pierre de Bourdeille, abbé de 51, 62
Brutus, Lucius Junius 47
Brutus, Marcus Junius 47, 49, 50
Bullingbrook, Henry (Duke of Lancaster) *see* Henry IV (King of England)
Bullough, Geoffrey 2, 4

Caesar, Julius 10–11, 30, 46–51, 60n.16, 60n.18, 60n.19, 60n.20
Calvin, Jean 74
Capet, Hugh [Hugues] (King of France) 11
Cartwright, Kent 96n.39
Cazaux, Yves 95n.25
Chaintron, Maria 60n.21
Chaix, Paul 15n.8
Champier, Symphorien 62
Chantelouve, François de (*La tragédie de feu Gaspard de Colligny*) 42–45, 46, 52, 55–57, 58, 59n.11, 59n.12, 59–60n.15, 60n.17, 77
Chapman, George 7, 14n.5, 31n.5
Charlemagne 11
Charles V (Holy Roman Emperor) 49
Charles IX (King of France) 60n.20
Châtillon *see* Coligny
Cinthio, Giambattista Giraldi
  Hecatommithi, Gli 66, 76, 77
  Orbecce 37, 58n.4
Claudian [Claudius Claudianus] (*In Rufinum*) 52–56 *passim*, 61n.26, 61n.28
Clément, Jacques 94n.23
Cleopatra (Queen of Egypt) 74
Coligny, Gaspard de (also Châtillon) 39, 41, 42, 46, 47, 52, 55, 59n.9, 59n.10, 60n.17, 61n.28, 61n.29, 78
Condé, Henri I de Bourbon, Prince of 60n.20
Corneille, Pierre 6

Courgenay, Claude Billard de *see* Billard de Courgenay
Cox, John D. 58n.3
Craigie, James 64, 93n.14
Crouzet, Denis 12–13, 15n.16, 59n.10, 60n.20
Cunningham, J. S. 59n.13, 79, 80, 87, 93n.17, 95n.30

Daniel, Samuel
  Civile Wars, The 17, 21, 24
  Cleopatra 37
  Philotas 37
Death of Herod, The (N. Town plays) 35, 36
Deierhauf-Holsboer, S. Wilma 6, 15n.18
Descartes, René 18
De Somogyi, Nick 65, 68, 80–81, 93n.3, 93n.8, 93n.10, 96n.33
Devereux, Robert *see* Essex
Donaldson, Ian 61n.24
Donne, John (*Devotions*) 12
Drummond, William [of Hawthornden] 60–61n.24
Du Bartas, Guillaume de Salluste, seigneur 60n.24, 64, 83, 86, 88, 89, 91, 92, 93n.14, 96n.34
  Judit, La 53–56, 61n.26, 61n.27, 63–75 *passim*, 81–86, 93n.14, 96n.34
Du Bellay, Martin 62
Dufour, Alain 15n.8
Duplessis-Mornay *see* Mornay, Philippe de, seigneur du Plessis-Marly
Du Rosier, Pierre (*Déploration de la France*) 39–40, 41, 42, 43, 44, 52, 58n.6, 58–59n.7, 59n.12, 78
Du Verdier, Antoine, seigneur de Vauprivaz 79, 95n.27

Edward II (King of England) 19
Elizabeth I (Queen of England) 20, 63
Ellis-Fermor, Una M. 95n.26

Index

Épernon, Jean-Louis de Nogaret de La Valette, Duke of 19, 32n.11, 46
Epicurus 52, 60n.22
Essex, Robert Devereux, Earl of 10, 15n.12, 19, 20–21

Fleury, Antoine (*Responce à un certain escrit*) 41–42, 47, 57
Florio, John (translator of Montaigne's *Essais*) 47
Fonteny, Jacques de (*Cléophon*) 94n.23
Forker, Charles R. 17–18
Fortescue, Thomas (*The Foreste*) 79, 84, 87, 90, 95n.27, 95n.28, 95n.29, 96n.38
Freud, Sigmund 93n.12
Fronton Du Duc (*L'histoire tragique de la Pucelle de Dom-Rémy*) 78

Garnier, Robert 37, 39
   Cornélie 38, 47–48, 51, 60n.17
   Marc Antoine 37
   Porcie 38, 39, 42
Gaveston, Piers [Pieres de Gabaston] (Earl of Cornwall) 19
Gibbon, Charles (*A watch-worde for warre*) 65
Gibbons, Brian 77
Giraldi, Giambattista *see* Cinthio
Gloucester, Thomas of Woodstock, Duke of *see* Woodstock, Thomas of
Godefroy de Bouillon *see* Bouillon, Godefroy de
Gontaut, Charles de *see* Biron
Gorboduc see Sackville, Thomas, and Thomas Norton
Goulart, Simon 9, 14–15n.8, 63
   Histoire des choses mémorables avenues en France 14–15n.8
   historical collection, of the most memorable accidents, etc., An 9, 10, 11, 14n.7, 15n.9, 15n.11
   troisiesme recveil, Le 15n.13

Gournay, Marie le Jars de (*Le promenoir de Monsieur de Montaigne*) 94n.18
Greenblatt, Stephen J. 34, 44
Greene, Robert (*Perimedes the Blacksmith*) 94n.24
Greville, Fulke 37
Grévin, Jacques (*César*) 50, 51
Gruget, Claude (translator of Pedro Mexía) 78–79, 84, 87, 90, 95n.25, 95n.26, 95n.27, 95n.28, 95n.29, 96n.37, 96n.38
Guise, François, Duke of *see* Lorraine, François de
Guise, Henri, Duke of *see* Lorraine, Henri de
Guise, Louis, Cardinal of *see* Lorraine, Louis, Cardinal of
Gundel, Philipp 52

Harington, John (translator of Ariosto, *Orlando Furioso*) 75–77, 94n.19, 94n.20
Helgerson, Richard 4
Henri III (King of France) 10, 18, 19, 21, 23, 24, 27, 29, 51, 59n.9, 60n.21, 94n.23
Henri IV (King of France and Navarre) 3, 4, 5, 9, 19, 20, 50, 59n.9, 94n.23
Henry IV (King of England) 11, 28
Herbert, Mary Sidney, Countess of Pembroke 37
Herford, C. H., Percy Simpson and Evelyn Simpson (eds of Ben Jonson) 60n.23
Heyns, Pieter (*Le miroir des vefves*) 63
Histoire des cinq rois see Goulart, Simon, *Histoire des choses mémorables avenues en France*
historical collection, of the most memorable accidents, and tragicall massacres of France, An see Goulart, Simon; Matthieu, Pierre

Holinshed, Raphael (*et al.*) (*Chronicles*) 9, 14n.6, 24, 28, 32n.9, 66, 81
Holstein, Hugo 93n.13
Holy League *see* Sainte Ligue
Honigmann, E. A. J. 93n.15
Hotman, François (*La Gavle Françoise* [*Francogallica*]) 49
Hudson, James 64
Hudson, Thomas (translator of Du Bartas, *La Judit*) 54, 61n.26, 63–64, 72, 74, 75, 86, 93n.14, 96n.34
Hurault, Michel
discourse vpon the present estate of France, A 10, 15n.13, 48
excellent discourse vpon the now present estate of France, An 11
Excellent et libre discours, sur l'estat present de la France 15n.13

Izard, Thomas C. 95n.28, 95n.29

Jacobus, Mary 93n.12
James VI (King of Scotland; later James I of England) 64
Jeanne d'Arc 66, 78
John, Don [of Austria] 63
Jones, Leonard Chester 14–15n.8
Jonson, Ben 60n.24
Epigrammes (132) 60n.24
Sejanus 52–58, 61n.25, 61n.26, 61n.30, 61n.31
Volpone 67
Jouanna, Arlette 59n.9, 61n.27
Julius Caesar *see* Caesar, Julius

Kelley, Donald R. 15n.15
Kibbee, Douglas A. 15n.17
Killing of Abel, The (Wakefield plays) 36
King, Ros 15n.10
Kingdon, Robert 14n.8

Kocher, Paul H. 77, 80
Kyd, Thomas
Cornelia (translation of Robert Garnier, *Cornélie*) 38, 47–48
Spanish Tragedy, The 33–34, 35, 40, 42, 52

Lacan, Jacques 2
Lacroix, Paul 6
Lancaster, House of 11, 21, 23
Languet, Hubert 47
La Noue, François de 62
Laroque, François 81–82
Last Judgement, The (Wakefield plays) 35
Lauvergnat-Gagnière, Christiane 59n.8, 59n.9
Lawrence, Jason 15n.17
Lazard, Madeleine 6
League, Holy *see* Sainte Ligue
L'Estoile, Pierre de (*Registre-Journal*) 48–49
Lodge, Thomas (*The Wounds of Civil War*) 58n.5
Lorraine, Charles de, Duke of Mayenne 11, 20
Lorraine, François de, Duke of Guise 21, 49, 55, 63
Lorraine, Henri de, Duke of Guise 6, 10–11, 15n.12, 18, 19–20, 21, 29, 46, 48–49, 50, 51, 60n.19, 60n.21, 64
Lorraine, House of 11
Lorraine, Louis, Cardinal of (also Cardinal of Guise) 6, 18, 19, 48–49
Louis XII (King of France) 51
Lucan [Marcus Annaeus Lucanus] 39
Luther, Martin 72, 93n.13
Lydgate, John (*The Fall of Princes*) 17
Lyly, John (*Campaspe*) 86, 88, 91, 96n.38

Index

Machiavelli, Nicolò [Machiavelism, Machiavellian characters] 20, 27, 41, 42, 45, 46, 48, 53, 56, 58, 77, 88, 91
Macintire, Elizabeth Jelliffe 36–37
Mareschal, André (*La cour bergère*) 7
Marguerite de Navarre (*Heptaméron*) 95n.25
Marius, Caius 58n.5
Marlowe, Christopher 13, 37, 47, 62, 82
   Doctor Faustus 43, 44, 59n.14
   Edward II 17, 19–20, 21
   Jew of Malta, The 34–35, 36, 41, 46, 48, 95n.26
   Massacre at Paris, The 6, 13, 19, 20, 21, 29–30, 31n.4, 32n.11, 46, 47, 48, 60n.18, 60n.19, 63, 77
   Tamburlaine 8, 41, 43, 59n.13, 63, 65, 75, 77–92, 93n.17, 94n.24, 95n.26, 95n.28, 95n.29, 95n.30, 95n.31, 96n.32, 96n.35, 96n.37
Marston, John (*Antonio's Revenge*) 33
Mary, Queen of Scots 15n.9
Matthieu, Pierre 5, 18–19
   Guisiade, La 5, 10, 15n.11, 16–31, 31n.1, 31n.2, 31n.7, 31–32n.8, 32n.10, 32n.11, 45–46, 49–50
   Histoire des derniers troubles de France 9, 10, 15n.9, 15n.11, 29
   historical collection, of the most memorable accidents, etc., An 9, 10, 11
   see also Goulart, Simon
Mayenne, Duke of *see* Lorraine, Charles de
Medici, Catherine de (Queen, then regent, of France) 19–20
Mexía, Pedro (*Silva de varia leccion*) 78–79, 84, 87, 90, 95n.26, 95n.27, 95n.28, 95n.29, 96n.37, 96n.38
Michel, Estienne 95n.27
Miola, Robert S. 58n.3, 73
Mirror for Magistrates, The 17
Moeckli, Gustave 15n.8
'Monarchomachs' 47

Monluc, Blaise de (*Commentaires*) 62, 92n.1
Montaigne, Michel Eyquem de (*Essais*) 47, 60n.16
Montpensier, Catherine Marie de Lorraine, Duchess of (sister of Henri de Lorraine, Duke of Guise) 60n.21
Montreux, Nicolas de ['Ollenix du Mont-Sacré']
   Cléopâtre, La tragédie de 3
   Diane, La, Pastourelle ou Fable Bosquagere 14n.3
   Isabelle, La tragédie d' 76–77, 94n.22
Mornay, Phillippe de, seigneur du Plessis-Marly 47, 62
Moysson, Iaqves 58n.6
Muret, Marc-Antoine (*Iulius Caesar*) 51

Navarre, Henri de *see* Henri IV (King of France and Navarre)
Navarre, King of *see* Bourbon, Antoine de; Henri IV (King of France and Navarre)
Navarre, Queen of *see* Albret, Jeanne d'; Marguerite de Navarre
Neill, Michael 4
Nemours, Anne d'Este, Duchess of (mother of Henri de Lorraine, Duke of Guise) 51, 60n.21
Noble, Richmond 93n.15
Nogaret de La Valette *see* Épernon
Norris, John 19
North, Thomas 11
Norton, Thomas *see* Sackville, Thomas, and Thomas Norton (*Gorboduc*)

Oliver, H. J. 31n.4, 60n.19
Ortelius, Abraham (cartographer) 80, 96n.32

Parthenay, Catherine de (*Holoferne*) 63
Patterson, Annabel 15n.12

Peele, George (*David and Bethsabe*) 81, 96n.33
Pellissier, Georges 94n.22
Pembroke, Countess of *see* Herbert, Mary Sidney
Perondinus, Petrus (*Magni Tamerlanis Scythiarum Imperatoris Vita*) 79, 95n.26
Philip II (King of Spain) 63
Plutarch (*Lives*) 10, 11, 46, 50
Poltrot de Méré, Jean 61n.27
Pompey (Gnaeus Pompeius Magnus) 51, 60n.20
Preston, Thomas (*Cambyses*) 38

Rabelais, François 71
Racine, Jean 6
Rich, Townsend 94n.19, 94n.20
Richard II (King of England) 21
Riffaterre, Michael 14n.4
Ronsard, Pierre de 39
  Franciade, La 38
Rossiter, A. P. 31n.6
Rowse, A. L. 13
Rufinus, Flavius (minister of the Eastern Roman emperor) 57

Sackville, Thomas, and Thomas Norton (*Gorboduc*) 37, 38
Sainte Ligue 5, 6, 9, 10, 11, 18, 19, 21, 27, 31, 32n.11
Seaton, Ethel 95n.26, 96n.32
Seneca, Lucius Annaeus 16, 18, 33–58 *passim*, 58n.3, 58n.4, 61n.30, 73
  Agamemnon 43
  Epistulae Morales 52, 60n.22
  Thyestes 43, 44
Serres, Jean de 9
Shaheen, Naseeb 93n.11, 93n.15
Shakespeare, Judith 71
Shakespeare, Susanna 71
Shakespeare, William 2, 3, 5, 6, 19, 27, 31, 62, 71, 82, 93n.11

All's Well That Ends Well 12, 68, 93n.8
Antony and Cleopatra 12, 16, 17, 68, 70, 76
Coriolanus 17, 67, 68
First Tetralogy 17, 21
Hamlet 3–4, 16, 17, 34, 36, 40, 44
Henry IV, Part 1 17, 68
Henry IV, Part 2 68, 80, 93n.11, 95n.31
Henry V 8–9, 10, 11, 15n.12, 68, 80, 88, 93n.11
Henry VI, Part 1 66
Henry VI, Part 3 93n.11
Julius Caesar 10–11, 46, 47, 48, 51, 60n.19
King John 93n.11
King Lear 16, 17, 35
Love's Labour's Lost 70, 71, 93n.10
Macbeth 17, 22, 36, 68, 81
Measure for Measure 75, 93n.16
Midsummer Night's Dream, A 14n.3, 94n.18
Othello 16, 17, 63, 65, 66–77, 81, 88, 93n.8, 93n.13, 93n.15, 94n.21
Richard II 5, 16–31
Richard III 36, 41, 42, 58n.1
Romeo and Juliet 17
Second Tetralogy 17
Titus Andronicus 34, 58n.3
Winter's Tale, The 74
Shepard, Alan 77–78
Shepherd, Simon 60n.18, 88
Sidney, Philip 37
  Apology for Poetry, An 37
  Arcadia 7
Simonini, Rinaldo C. 15n.17
Simpson, Evelyn *see* Herford, C. H., *et al.*
Simpson, Percy *see* Herford, C. H., *et al.*
Sixtus V (Pope) 20
Sokol, B. J. 93n.9
Spenser, Edmund (*The Faerie Queene*) 70

Street, J. S. 93n.2
Stuart, Mary *see* Mary, Queen of Scots
Sulla [Lucius Sulla Felix] 58n.5
Sylvester, Josuah (translator of Du Bartas) 60n.24, 72, 93n.14

Taillemont, Claude de (*Discours des champs faëz*) 93–94n.18
Tamburlaine (Emir of the Timurid Empire) *see* Timur
Tarquinius Superbus, Lucius (King of Rome) 47
Tavannes, Gaspard de Saulx, seigneur de 62
Theodosius I (Emperor of the Eastern Roman Empire) 52
Timur ['Tamburlaine', 'Tamerlane'] (Emir of the Timurid Empire) 39, 41, 77–79, 80, 96n.37
tocsin contre les massacreurs et avteurs des confusions en France, Le 61n.28
Townshend, Roger 92n.1
tragédie française du bon Kanut, roi de Danemark, La 40–41, 59n.8, 59n.9

Ugoleto, Taddeo 52

Valois, House of 19
Vauprivaz *see* Du Verdier, Antoine
Vauquelin de La Fresnaye, Jean (*L'art poétique*) 94n.22
Vautrollier, Thomas 63–64
Vieilleville, François de Scepeaux, sire de 62
Vindiciae contra tyrannos (by 'Stephanus Junius Brutus') 47

Webster, John (*The Duchess of Malfi*) 36
Weil, Judith 13, 60n.18, 77
Whetstone, George
 English Myrror, The 79, 84, 87, 90, 95n.28, 95n.29, 96n.37
 Heptameron 93n.16
Woodstock (anonymous play) 17, 21–22, 23, 31n.6
Woodstock, Thomas of (Duke of Gloucester) 21, 25

Yates, Frances 15n.17